The Entire World of SH & CH™ Instructional Workbook

By

Christine Ristuccia M.S., CCC-SLP

and

Jim Ristuccia

(760) 613-6760
www.sayitright.org

Duplicating

ISBN 0-9760490-1-5

Say It Right™
(760) 613-6760
www.sayitright.org

About the Authors

Christine Ristuccia, M.S., CCC-SLP, received her master of science degree in communicative disorders at the University of Redlands, Redlands, CA and a bachelor of science degree in health science from San Diego State University.

Ms. Ristuccia is an experienced school-based speech-language pathologist, and has worked with a wide range of communicative disorders ranging from preschool through adulthood. She is a frequent speaker at state and national speech and hearing organization meetings.

Jim Ristuccia, M.S., is a graduate of Villanova University, Villanova, PA and the Joint Military Intelligence College, Washington, DC. He has been instrumental in the creation and development of all **Say It Right**™ products from the inception of the company.

Say It Right™, was founded in 1999 by Ms. Ristuccia. **Say It Right**™ develops and publishes clinically tested and fun to use educational teaching tools. The first product line, **The Entire World of R**™, an innovative product for teaching the eight variations of the /r/ phoneme, was released in 2000.

Table of Contents

Introduction

The number of resources available covering remediation of affricates and fricatives is limited, therefore similar to our other books, ***The Entire World of SH & CH***™ was written to fill a need in speech-pathology.

Our most important contribution, we feel, is an easy-to-follow strategy designed to help organize your therapy and approach toward remediation. Coupled with specific exercises to implement your therapeutic strategy, we hope you will find this the most comprehensive resource covering the four sibilant sounds: /ʃ/, /ʧ/, /ʤ/ and /ʒ/.

The foundation of our methodology is to build upon success with related phonemes to elicit success with other phonemes. Targeted exercises using approximate phonemic production zone assists are provided in each chapter. These exercises utilize producible sounds, such as employing /t/ in combination with /ʃ/ to produce /ʧ/ (e.g. nut shell becomes nutchell).

Each section, like our other Instructional Workbooks, include single words, phrases and sentences. Since the target remediation audience for affricates and fricatives is younger than for other sounds, the exercises are geared for a younger audience. The pictures of the target words are enlarged and colorable. There are even templates for students to cut out pictures and make "books" of their target words. This is intended to increase tactile and visual learning opportunities. Additionally, we've included more fun worksheets to help keep your students motivated for improved speech production.

We hope you enjoy!

Christine Ristuccia
Jim Ristuccia
Carlsbad, CA
February 2004

A Note About Phonetic Transcription

The International Phonetic Alphabet (IPA) prescribes a common linguistic means to describe sound so that it will be useful for speakers of any language and dialect to understand pronunciation. The proper phonetic transcription for sounds used in this book are:

sh	/ʃ/
ch	/ʧ/
j	/ʤ/
zh	/ʒ/
y	/j/
th	/θ/

The intended audience of this book while primarily for speech-language pathologists also includes students, classroom teachers, and parents. Complete use of the IPA for readers unfamiliar with phonetic transcription would be distracting and cumbersome. Therefore, in Chapters 5 through 7, which are designed for student use, the "English" equivalents (as shown above) are employed. This will aid in achieving our goal of facilitating better communication with the clients, parents and teachers.

CHAPTER 1:
Facts About:
/ʃ/, /ʒ/, /ʧ/ & /ʤ/

Facts About /ʃ/, /ʒ/, /ʧ/ & /ʤ/

The sibilant consonants--/ʃ/, /ʒ/, /ʧ/, and /ʤ/--are grouped together because of the similar nature in which they are produced and treated.

The sibilant nature or sibilancy of these sounds refers to the hissing sound which are common characteristics of /ʃ/, /ʒ/, /ʧ/ and /ʤ/ as well as the other related phonemes /s/ and /z/. One of the common characteristics of the sibilants is the high frequency level of the sound production. Compare the words, "mom" and "chew". Notice how the /m/ is much lower in frequency than the /ʧ/ in chew. Frequency ranges for the sibilants are higher than most other sounds and may be two to four times greater than for other sounds.

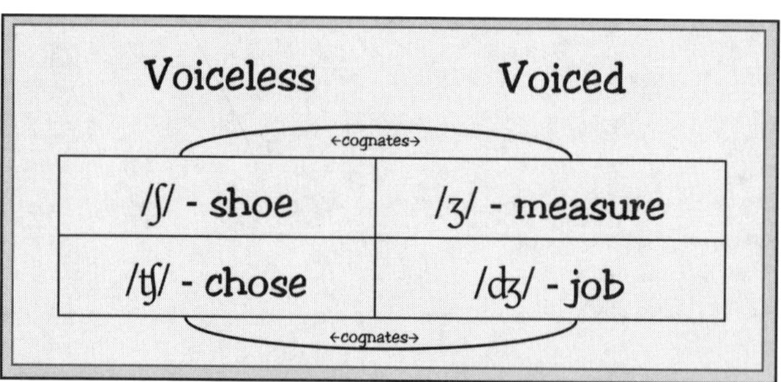

Voiceless	Voiced
/ʃ/ - shoe	/ʒ/ - measure
/ʧ/ - chose	/ʤ/ - job

Correct production of our four target phonemes (/ʃ/, /ʒ/, /ʧ/ and /ʤ/) are typically developed in children by four years of age. In some cases, the phoneme may be present as early as eighteen months of age. Deficiencies in production is most noticeable in infantile speech, but it may occur in children that have had a history of ear infections or suffer from a high frequency hearing loss.

Other deficiencies may be attributed to physiological defects, delayed speech, lateral lisp disorders, or phonetic substitution, most notable when combined with another consonant, such as in the word washed.

Palatal Production

The /ʧ/, /ʤ/, /ʃ/ and /ʒ/ phonemes are palatal sounds. The sounds are produced at the point of interaction between the tongue tip and the hard palate region.

The palatal region is the top arched section of the mouth, frequently referred to as the "roof of the mouth."

The posterior third of the palate is called the velum or soft palate. The anterior two-thirds or bony area is called the hard palate. The area immediately in front of the palate and behind the gum line of the upper central incisors is called the alveolar ridge region. The alveolar ridge is the point of production for many

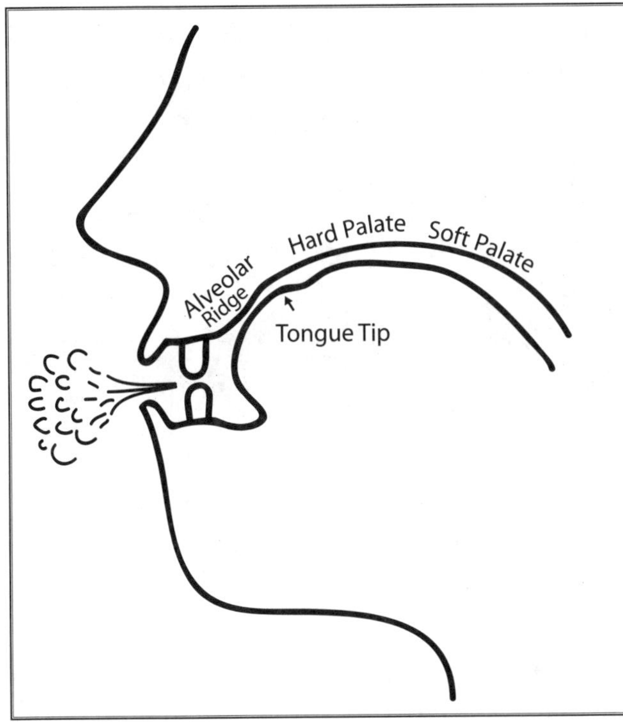

Figure 1-1 Parts of the mouth showing positioning for /ʃ/

sounds notably /s/ and /z/. In some instances, the point of production for the target sounds will be in front of the palate to the alveolar ridge. This is because the blade of the tongue will straddle both the alveolar ridge and the hard palate. In rare cases production can be as far forward as the *lower* central incisors. As long as pronunciation is correct, this production is acceptable. To broadly characterize the point of production for /ʧ/, /ʤ/, /ʃ/, and /ʒ/ the term palato-alveolar is often used. Figure 1-1 shows the major portions of the mouth involved in the productions of /ʧ/, /ʤ/, /ʃ/, and /ʒ/.

Sound is created at the palatal region as a result of airflow emitting from the vocal tract over the tongue and between the palate. The close interaction of the tongue and mouth results in the subject sounds.

Characteristics of /ʃ/ and /ʒ/

The /ʃ/ and /ʒ/ (as in ***sh***ip and mea***s***ure) phonemes are produced in the same manner and are considered to be cognates (related by similar nature and quality). The /ʃ/ is unvoiced, while the /ʒ/ is voiced (with vocal cord vibration).

Both /ʃ/ and /ʒ/ are regarded as continuant fricative sibilants due to the continuous stream of airflow required to produce both sounds, the manner in which the sound is produced, and the characteristic of the sound emitted. *Continuant* refers to the steady stream of airflow. *Fricative* refers to the friction produced between the palatal region and the tongue. And, *sibilant* to the distinctive hissing sound made during production.

To produce the /ʃ/ and /ʒ/, the front portion of the tongue is elevated and approximated (not touching) toward the hard palate or palato-alveolar region. The lateral portions of the tongue are pressed against the upper back teeth. A breath is expelled centrally and sustained. The teeth are slightly separated, and the lips are protruded slightly and drawn at the corners. The vocal cords do not vibrate for /ʃ/, but do vibrate for /ʒ/.

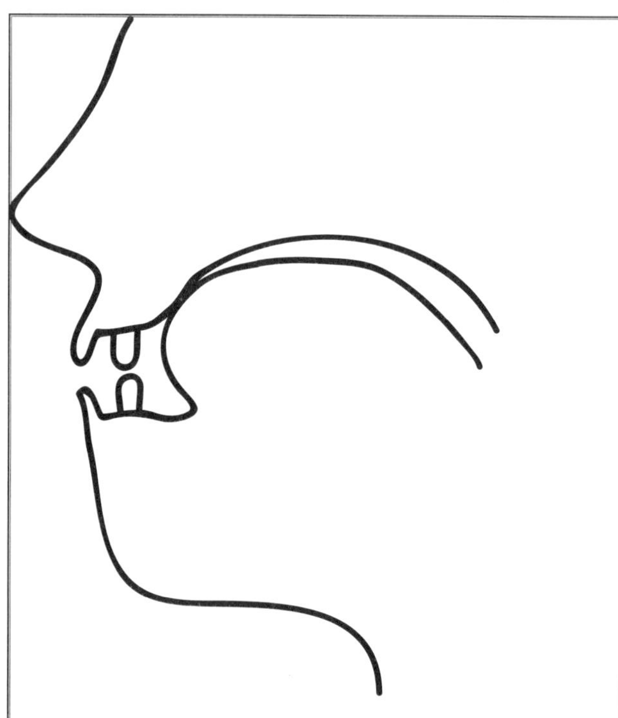

Figure 1-2 *Mouth positioning for /ʧ/ and /ʤ/ showing interruption of airflow.*

Characteristics of /ʧ/ and /ʤ/

The /ʧ/ and /ʤ/ (as in ***ch***op and ju***dge)*** are also cognates, since they are produced in the same position with voicing being the only difference. The /ʧ/ is unvoiced while the /ʤ/ is voiced (with vocal cord vibration).

Both /ʧ/ and /ʤ/ are traditionally called *affricates* or stop-plosive *fricatives* since airflow is completely closed at a given point in the vocal tract at the initiation of the sound (stop), then followed by a release of air (plosive) through a narrow opening in the mouth (Figures 1-2 and 1-3).

The /ʧ/ is really a combination of /t/ and /ʃ/. The /t/ is the stop-plosive and /ʃ/ the fricative. Similarly, the /ʤ/ is a combination of /d/ and /ʒ/. The /d/ and /ʒ/ being the voiced cognates to /t/ and /ʃ/.

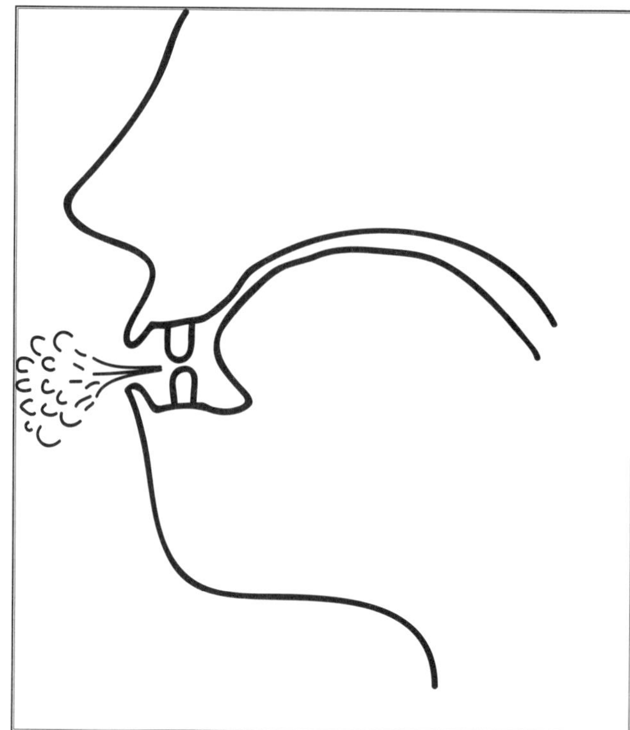

Figure 1-3 *Mouth positioning for /ʧ/ and /ʤ/ showing the plosive release phase.*

The phonemes are produced as the tongue is raised and placed in contact with the palato-alveolar region at a point slightly posterior to where a /t/ is produced (upper front incisors to alveolar ridge). The tip of the tongue touches the palato-alveolar ridge. The teeth are nearly closed. Breath is held momentarily (stop) and then quickly released with the tongue tip (plosive release). The lips are slightly protruded and rounded. As the breath escapes, an explosive, staccato sound is created. The vocal cords do not vibrate for /ʧ/, but do vibrate for /ʤ/.

Due to the abrupt start and tense nature of the production of the sound(s), the duration of /ʧ/ and /ʤ/ phonemes are much shorter than

/ʧ/ Different Spelling, Same Pronunciation

Ch as in church
T as in picture

/ʃ/ Different Spelling, Same Pronunciation

Sh as in shop
Ci as in sufficient
S as in sugar
Ti as in rational
Ch as in Charlotte
Ss as in tissue

/ʤ/ Different Spelling, Same Pronunciation

J as in jump
G as in passage
Dge as in fudge
Di as in soldier

/ʒ/ Different Spelling, Same Pronunciation

S as in closure
Si as in occasion
G as in beige
J as in bijou
X as in luxury

Figure 1-4 *Spelling variations*

that of other sounds.

Spelling

As with most sounds in the English language, the spelling of a word is not necessarily a determinant for pronunciation. Figure 1-4 presents the multiple spelling variations that represent /ʧ/, /ʤ/, /ʃ/, and /ʒ/ phonemes. There are numerous spelling combinations for each of the sounds.

Definitions

Affricate: Complex sound production when slowly released. Stop consonants are followed immediately by fricatives at the same point of articulation.

Cognate: Having the same nature or quality.

Continuants: The continuation or uninterrupted stream of air from the lungs.

Fricative: Pronounced by forcing the breath, either voiced or voiceless, through a narrow slit formed at some point in the mouth.

Sibilant: A consonant characterized by a hissing sound.

Stop: Involves complete closure at any given point in the vocal tract.

Plosive: Sounds are made by forming a complete obstruction to the flow of air through the mouth and nose. The first stage is that a closure occurs. Next, the flow of air builds up and finally the closure is released, making an explosion of air that results in a sharp noise.

Figure 1-5 *Definitions*

The Entire World of SH & CH™ Strategy

The Entire World of SH & CH™ strategy is to evaluate and initially treat articulation disorders which affect the palatal consonants. This methodology uses phoneme combinations that are in the approximate phonemic production zone(s). By using phonemic combinations to elicit correct productions, placement and sound stabilization are achieved prior to targeting more difficult sound combinations. This approach leads to success.

The cornerstone of ***The Entire World of SH & CH™*** approach is to conduct a comprehensive evaluation of all four word positions--/ʃ/, /ʒ/, /ʧ/ & /ʤ/--and then treat the phonemes and word positions that are misproduced by the student. Finally, you can use the evaluation results to determine the remediation protocol.

Ultimately, the student's success is transferred, utilizing sound and word combinations that she can already produce to achieve more difficult and elusive /ʃ/, /ʒ/, /ʧ/ and /ʤ/ phonetic combinations.

CHAPTER 2: *Evaluation*

Evaluation

Understanding exactly what the student is capable of producing is critical for establishing an effective treatment plan. Most young students are able to quickly learn and produce the target phonemes once therapy is initiated. The key, however, is making therapy as productive as possible by focusing only on the misarticulated sounds.

Students are often able to produce one phoneme but not another (e.g. /ʧ/ but not /ʃ/). It is also valuable to know if the error(s) are consistent across all word positions, or isolated to one particular placement, such as the final word position. This information is important because it gives the instructor a starting point for therapy. You can use the student's success to facilitate the other target phonemes and/or word positions.

After establishing which sounds can and cannot be produced, the instructor is ready to develop goals and begin treatment.

The Entire World of SH & CH™ Screening Form is an excellent tool for discriminating the various sounds. The screening form aids in evaluating initial, medial and final word positions for /ʃ/, /ʧ/, and /ʤ/ phonemes, and the medial and final word positions for the /ʒ/ phoneme.

The phonemes /s/ and /z/ are included because as sibilant consonants they are closely related to /ʃ/ and /ʧ/. Several of the exercises in this book assume correct production of /s/ and /z/. Deficiencies and correction techniques with the /s/ and /z/ sounds are addressed in ***The Entire World of S & Z™ Instructional Workbook.***

The letter "H" is also evaluated because /ʧ/ final is contained in the pronunciation of the letter. Therefore, if the student can say "H," then they usually can say final /ʧ/. It is a "tricky" way of checking for /ʧ/ production.

The phoneme /j/ initial, as in **y**ellow, is also included on the screening form. As a palato-alveolar sound, /j/ is produced in a similar manner to the target sounds and thus can be used for several of the approximate phonemic production zone exercises. Correct pronunciation of /j/ is therefore required to perform the elicitation exercises in this book.

Student Name ____________________

Screening Date __________ Date of Birth __________

Examiner ____________________

Percentage Correct ____________________

SAY IT RIGHT™

The Entire World of SH & CH™ Screening Form

/ʧ/	**1. Initial /ʧ/** cherry, chair, chop (cherry)	**2. Medial /ʧ/** teacher, pitcher, kitchen (teacher)	**3. Final /ʧ/** lunch, beach, watch (lunch)
/ʤ/	**4. Initial /ʤ/** jump, jam, jet (jump)	**5. Medial /ʤ/** magic, vegetable, soldier (magic)	**6. Final /ʤ/** orange, cage, bridge (orange)
/ʃ/	**7. Initial /ʃ/** shoe, ship, shop (shoe)	**8. Medial /ʃ/** tissue, ocean, lotion (tissue)	**9. Final /ʃ/** fish, brush, wash (fish)
/ʒ/	The phoneme /ʒ/ does not occur in the initial position in the English language.	**10. Medial /ʒ/** treasure, Asia, television (treasure)	**11. Final /ʒ/** garage, beige, collage (garage)
/s/	**12. Initial /s/** circle, sand, soap (circle)	**13. Medial /s/** insect, lasso, recipe (insect)	**14. Final /s/** horse, tennis, race (horse)
/z/	**15. Initial /z/** zero, zoo, xylophone (zero)	**16. Medial /z/** jersey, newspaper, music (jersey)	**17. Final /z/** cards, birds, games (cards)

18. Initial /h/ spell the word "h i g h" (H)	**19. Initial /j/** yo-yo, yellow, yes (yo-yo)

www.sayitright.org

Figure 2-1 *Screening Form*

How to Use *The Entire World of SH & CH*™ Screening Form

Instruct the student to produce each phoneme. If the student doesn't know the name of a picture, tell her the name and skip to the next stimulus card. Continue with the next two to three words then return to the unknown word. This is to ensure a pure production from the student.

Next, determine eligibility for services relative to age, ability, and maturity.

The evaluation form can also be used to specifically investigate which target phoneme(s) the student continues to misproduce even after she has received speech and language therapy.

Once a baseline is established for the student, the therapist is ready to develop remediation goals and begin treatment.

The results from the evaluation are used to determine which treatment protocol to use. The "Remediation Protocol Options" chart found on page 24, lists the three main outcomes from the evaluation form. Each outcome has a corresponding elicitation technique that is discussed in detail in Chapter 3, "Treatment."

CHAPTER 3: *Treatment*

Where to Begin

➤ Establish a comprehensive baseline by using ***The Entire World of SH & CH™ Screening Form***. Determine the results and follow the evaluation outcome options in this section.

➤ Consistently practice the deviant /ʃ/, /ʒ/, /ʧ/ and /ʤ/ phonemes and word positions until mastery is achieved. An 80% correct response rate at the sentence level is recommended.

➤ Use success in one word position to shape another word position. For example the phrase, "ten ships" begins with an /n/ final word (ten); however, by combining the phrase to "tenships", it turns into a /ʧ/ medial word.

➤ Use successful productions of phonemes in the general pronunciation area. The phonemes /t/, /s/, /d/, /n/ and /j/ are all created near the palatal region of the mouth (either at the alveolar ridge or hard palate) and are phonemes that most students can already produce. Use success with these phonemes to elicit correct placement and pronunciation of /ʃ/, /ʒ/, /ʧ/, and /ʤ/.

➤ For optimal success, incorporate all the principles from this book when performing therapy.

➤ For carry-over activities, combine exercises from this book with ***The Entire World of SH & CH™ Book of Stories***.

How to Use The Entire World of SH & CH™ Instructional Workbook

Step 1: Evaluation

First, determine the nature of the disorder by using ***The Entire World of SH & CH™ Screening Form*** found in Chapter 2. Establish which specific /ʃ/, /ʒ/, /ʧ/ and /ʤ/ sounds the student can and cannot produce.

Step 2: Interpret the Evaluation Results

Use the results from the evaluation to probe problem areas. Usually students will have difficulty with most of the /ʃ/, /ʒ/, /ʧ/ & /ʤ/ variations. However, some students are able to produce a /ʃ/ and not a /ʧ/ or vice versa. From the evaluation results, a treatment plan using select target sounds can be developed. Keep in mind that each student is unique and the trained speech-language pathologist should adjust the treatment protocol as necessary.

Step 3: Kinesthetic Awareness

Kinesthetic refers to the sensation of position and movement of the tongue in the mouth. The student must have an awareness and reference point as to the location of his tongue when producing a sound to be successful in the exercises. To develop this awareness, ask the student where his tongue is when making or producing a correct /ʃ/ or /ʧ/ sound. If the student has no correct /ʃ/ or /ʧ/ productions, skip this step and revert back to the previous exercises.

Step 4: Phonemic Awareness

Phonemic awareness or ear training refers to the student's ability to hear the distinction between phonemes. This skill is important so that the student is able to distinguish a correct sound in order to produce it. This awareness can be taught at any stage during the remediation process. However, it is optimal to introduce correctly produced phonemes as early as possible.

Choose a word, phrase, or sentence list, and read the list to the student. Instruct him to listen and raise his hand when he hears the target sound(s). Use the contrast exercises found on pages 112, 142 and 143 to reinforce phonemic awareness skills.

Step 5: Begin Remediation

The result of the evaluation is the starting point for remediation. There are different elicitation techniques to use depending upon the mispro-duced phonemes.

Based on the results from ***The Entire World of SH & CH™ Screening Form***, determine a recommended course of action on beginning on page 23.

There are three main outcomes that will occur based on the screening results:

1. All four target phonemes: /ʃ/, /ʒ/, /ʧ/ and /ʤ/ are misarticulated.
2. /ʧ/ and /ʤ/ are misarticulated.
3. /ʃ/ and /ʒ/ are misarticulated.

Each action uses combination clusters to approximate the target sounds. For example, to obtain a /ʧ/ medial word position combine a /t/ final word with a /j/ initial word, such as "get you." Producing the combination together results medial /ʧ/ production. Obtaining success in one word position will often lead to success in the other word positions.

Specific exercises and techniques are found in the designated chapter(s) for that particular phoneme. The exercises were designed to be picked and chosen based on the needs of the student(s).

In my experience, none of the /ʃ/, /ʒ/, /ʧ/ and /ʤ/ phonemes are easier to produce than the others. Begin with the phoneme that the student is most stimulable for. If the student can not produce any of the sounds, then more probe testing needs to be done utilizing the elicitation techniques provided in this book. Over 98% of students are able to produce at least one of the target sounds in some capacity; continue to probe until you find a phoneme to build upon.

Step 6: Auditory, Tactile and Visual Cues

Cueing involves the creation of an association between a target sound and a particular object, sensation, or noise. The association is designed to trigger or enhance the ability to perform in a certain way or recall a certain experience. By "associating" target sounds with specific tactile, auditory or visual sensations, we attempt to enhance production.

Auditory cues link target sounds with common sounds or noises that the student is already familiar with. For example, referring to /ʧ/ as the "choo choo" sound provides visual and auditory cues for the student.

Even if the student cannot produce /ʧ/, he will know how it sounds.

Tactile sensation is being able to "feel" how the letter is formed in the mouth using as many senses as possible. Examples of tactile exercises include hand gestures, writing, tracing and/or coloring a letter while producing the sound(s). These cues greatly enhance the learning process.

Visual cueing involves a visual reference, such as putting a copy of the large "CH" picture on page 55, in front of the student while he says the sound. Visual gestures, pictures, and mouth diagrams also aid in visual association(s) with the sound. A mirror is particularly helpful for visual cueing to show lip, mouth, and tongue positioning.

Step 7: Initial, Medial and Final Word Positions

Don't be compelled to follow this book in any order. Just because the initial position appears first in the chapters doesn't mean that therapy should begin with the initial word position. In many cases the final or medial positions may be easier for your students to produce due to co-articulation/stimulability. In other cases, the student may have more success with the initial word position. Use the student's successful production of any word position to develop success in other word positions.

Remediation Hierarchy

Isolation
Word Level
Phrase Level
Sentence Level
Reading Aloud
Structured Conversation
Conversational Speech

Figure 3-1 *Remediation Hierarchy*

Step 8: Follow a Remediation Hierarchy

The Entire World of SH & CH™ program is designed to introduce student to isolation and word levels. These levels are the most basic. The program progresses through increasingly more difficult levels. See Figure 3-1 for the remediation hierarchy. In your therapy, build upon the student's success. Repeat and review previous exercises as necessary to enhance learning and maintain motivation.

Progress through all word positions. If student has difficulty, review the previously successful exercises.

Step 9: Structured Conversational Activities

The goal for the student is to self-monitor during conversational speech. Place your student in situations to practice. Reading aloud, a dialogue initiated by the instructor and games all create structured conversational activities which practice production.

Step 10: Review and Reinforcement

Review previously learned exercises at the beginning and end of each therapy session. Review as necessary to maintain proficiency.

Tips for Transferring Successful Elicitation from One Word Position to Another

What's the big deal about word position? Often times students are able to say a phoneme in one word position, but not another. Most likely it has to do with co-articulation, such as the /n/ in "inch" being so closely related to mouth and tongue position for /ʧ/ (thus making "inch" easier to pronounce than other /ʧ/ final words). Or, it could be related to consonant clusters which are around the phoneme. Some clusters, such as the /w/ in "wash" or "watch" are more difficult to produce based on motor planning or processing ability.

The techniques in this section implement ***The Entire World of SH & CH***™ strategy. These concepts are the foundation for the worksheets found in this book.

One of the main techniques in the book is to elicit specific word positions from other successfully produced word positions. The foundation of our strategy is to achieve success built upon by previous successes.

During the evaluation process mark the specific word positions that are produced correctly. Using these words can accelerate therapy. This approach will provide consistent practice for the student and enable him to clearly understand his goals. And finally, it will assist the student to achieve mastery.

To attain the best results and accelerate your remediation, use these methods for achieving approximate phonemic transfer:

➢ *First, combine correct final and initial word positions to create misarticulated medial word positions*. Even if the words don't make sense, the point is correct production of the target phoneme(s). Elongate the production of the sound to transfer word production. For example, if the student can successfully produce /ʃ/ final words, (e.g. bru**sh** or tra**sh**) then combine /ʃ/ final with an /ʃ/ initial word (e.g. bru**sh** **sh**op) to create a /ʃ/ medial word. The combined word bru**sh**op should be produced as brushhhhhop. Repeat several times until the sound is mastered at normal speed.

➢ *Second, transfer successful production of final and medial words to the initial position.* Also, isolate the sound immediately after successful production. Using the above example of brush shop, the successful production of /ʃ/ final is elongated to make a medial word: brushop. To create the initial position word, separate the initial (shop) from the medial combination word (brushop). Instruct the student to say the word brushop, pause, then say the initial word (shop) immediately following. In several of the exercises in the book, we use the "⇨" symbol to denote pausing and the creation of a new phoneme from the combined phoneme.

To build upon kinesthetic awareness, emphasize the phoneme by elongating the /ʃ/ bridge, (e.g. brushhhhhhop). Encourage the student to maintain his tongue and mouth position(s) when producing shop" while remembering how the mouth and tongue were positioned while saying "brush." Immediately recreate correct positioning when eliciting the /ʃ/ in isolation, "shop." If the student is unable to produce /ʃ/ initial, review the previous step (i.e. brush shop). Repeat the /ʃ/ medial exercise and try again.

➢ *Finally, to transfer successful production of medial words to the final position, use the whisper technique.* Ask the student to say a word containing the target phoneme that the student has correctly produced (e.g. marshmallow). Next instruct the student to repeat the word except this time pause between the medial and final portions of the word (e.g. marsh (pause) mallow). Finally, instruct the student to say the word again and pause in the middle, only this time whisper the final portion of the word. For example, say marsh and whisper *mallow,* separating the "marsh" from the "mallow." Repeat with other words.

Evaluation Outcomes and Recommended Courses of Action

Obtaining an accurate evaluation is critical for developing a proper treatment protocol.

Each student may present unique challenges to the instructor. Therefore, all treatment must be tailored to suit the particular needs of the student. There are several common articulation screening results that may occur when utilizing ***The Entire World of SH & CH™ Screening Form***. Those results are presented as "evaluation outcomes" on page 24, and suggest a recommended course of treatment.

Each chapter addresses one of the four target phonemes, yet the worksheets contained in each chapter do not indicate the order of treatment due to the uniqueness of each student.

From the possible evaluation outcomes (See Figure 3-2 Remediation Protocol Options on page 24), follow the recommended treatment exercises.

Intervention will involve use of word cluster combinations. These combinations take advantage of *approximate phonemic production zone assists* to elicit correct production of the target phonemes. For example, final /t/ is a good phonemic approximation for the initiation of the affricate /ʧ/. The phoneme /t/ is produced at the alveolar ridge and is a stop-plosive similar to /ʧ/. Combine a final /t/ word, such as "get", with an initial /j/ word, such as "you" and you can create a combination medial /ʧ/ word, "ge**tch**ew." This creates word combinations for student practice.

To simplify activities for the students, Chapters 5 through 8 use the common English equivalents (i.e. sh, ch, dj, zh) in place of the phonetic symbols used by the International Phonetic Alphabet (IPA).

Treatment exercises begin at the phrase level and then progress to sentence level. Keep in mind that not all exercises may work. It may require some trial and error, and professional judgement on the part of the therapist. Most importantly, use what works for the student to build upon his success.

Remediation Protocol Options

	Screening Outcome	Approximate Phonemic Production Zone Elicitation Techniques: Technique	Example	Page
#1	All the sibilant sounds are misarticulated: /ʃ/, /ʒ/, /ʧ/, /ʤ/	1. T Final + Y Initial ⇨ CH Medial	*get you ⇨ getchou*	59
		2. S Final + Y Initial ⇨ SH Medial	*kiss you ⇨ kisshou*	146
#2	/ʧ/ and /ʤ/ are misarticulated */ʃ/ and /ʒ/ are produced correctly*	1. T Final + Y Initial ⇨ CH Medial	*get you ⇨ getchou*	59
		2. T Final + SH Initial ⇨ CH Medial	*bright shell ⇨ brightchell*	61
		3. N Final + SH Initial ⇨ CH Medial	*ten ships ⇨ tenchips*	63
		4. N Final + CH Initial ⇨ CH Medial	*sun chair ⇨ sunchair*	66
		5. N + CH Final ⇨ CH Final	*in ch ⇨ inch*	65
		6. D Final + Y Initial ⇨ J Medial	*read your ⇨ readjour*	103
		7. D Final + J Initial ⇨ J Medial	*plaid jacket ⇨ plaidjacket*	105
		8. J Final + J Initial ⇨ J Medial	*village gypsy ⇨ villagypsy*	108
#3	/ʃ/ and /ʒ/ are misarticulated */ʧ/ and /ʤ/ are produced correctly*	1. S Final + Y Initial ⇨ SH Medial	*kiss you ⇨ kisshou*	146
		2. CH Final + SH Initial ⇨ SH Medial	*Each shark ⇨ Eachshark*	149
		3. SH Final + SH Initial ⇨ SH Medial	*Spanish shampoo ⇨ Spanishampoo*	154

Figure 3-2 *Remediation Protocol Options*

Evaluation Outcome #1:

All four sounds /ʃ/, /ʒ/, /ʧ/ & /ʤ/ are misarticulated

If the result(s) from the evaluation indicate that the student can not properly produce any of the target sounds, do additional probe testing. In most cases, the student is stimulable for at least one of the target sounds. The challenge for the therapist is to figure out which sound the student can approximate. This will indicate where successful productions can be achieved.

Test stimulability for both /ʧ/ and /ʃ/ by using the following exercises. Try the different techniques and review the worksheets to determine which sounds the student is better able to produce. Use the results to initiate a remediation protocol.

I. Stimulability Testing for CH

There are several techniques to probe for the /ʧ/ phoneme. First try the combination:

/t/ Final + /j/ Initial ⇨ /ʧ/ Medial

Example: get + you ⇨ getchew

The exercise worksheet is found on page 59. The /ʧ/ sound is composed of the /t/ + /ʃ/. The /t/ is a stop-plosive consonant. Most students are able to produce it. Touch the alveolar ridge with the tongue tip, stop airflow, and hold momentarily. Release the air by pointing the tongue tip forward. The sound created is a /t/. The stop quality, where in the sound is initiated by releasing airflow, is the same for the /t/ as for the /ʧ/.

The second part of the equation is the /ʃ/ phoneme. Since the student was not able to produce the /ʃ/, we use a substitute. The /j/ as in "yes" or "yo-yo" is related to /ʃ/ and /ʧ/ since the place of articulation is also palatal. The /j/ is a gliding consonant and it's presence can even be detected somewhere between the /t/ and /ʃ/ components of the /ʧ/. The ending point of a /j/ is similar to the ending point of the /ʧ/. Most importantly, since most children can say /j/ words, the /j/ provides an excellent elicitation point.

The key for this exercise is to "trick" the student into producing the sound by rapidly repeating the sample phrase(s) to produce a medial /ʧ/. The student should end up saying something like this:

get you, getyou, getyou, getchyou, getchyou, getchou, getchhuu

If the /t/ Final + /j/ Initial combination doesn't work to elicit /ʧ/, ask the student to say *"nch"* words such as "i**nch**," "lu**nch**," or "ra**nch**." The /n/ places the tongue in the approximate production zone for /ʧ/. The exercise worksheet for this combination is found on page 65.

Alternatively, ask the student to say the letter "H." The letter "H" contains a final /ʧ/, but the student will not recognize it as such. He may be able to produce it without realizing it. If he is successful, begin with /ʧ/ final combination exercises.

Finally, ask the student, "What sound does a train make?" The student should say, "choo choo." The student may be able to produce the sound correctly if an appropriate stimulus is applied.

If the student is stimulable for /ʧ/, then review the various /ʧ/ and /ʤ/ exercises with the student as presented in Evaluation Outcome #2, found on page 28. If the student is not stimulable for /ʧ/, try the techniques for /ʃ/ below or refer to the therapeutic tips for /ʧ/ in Chapter 5.

II. Stimulability Testing for /ʃ/

To test stimulability for /ʃ/ try the combination:

/s/ Final + /j/ Initial ⇨ /ʧ/ Medial

Example: kiss + you ⇨ kisshoe

The exercise worksheet is found on page 146. The /s/ is a continuant fricative like the /ʃ/, except that when /s/ is produced the tongue is nearly touching the alveolar ridge instead of curled up and back toward the hard palate, as it is for /ʃ/. The /j/ phoneme as discussed previously is used as a phonemic approximator because it is a palatal sound and closely approximates /ʃ/ production. Instruct the student to repeat the combination rapidly to produce a medial /ʃ/ such as:

kiss you, kissyou, kissyou, kisshyou, kisshyou, kisshhou, kisshhhu

If the /s/ final + /j/ initial combination is not successful, try using something familiar to stimulate production. For example, ask the student, "What do you say when a baby is sleeping?" Or, "What do you say to keep someone quiet?" Answer: "Shhhhh". In some cases the response is automatic and thus the student is able to produce to sound.

If the student is stimulable for /ʃ/, review the various /ʃ/ and /ʒ/ exercises with the student as presented in Evaluation Outcome #3 on page 31.

If the student is not stimulable for /ʃ/, repeat the techniques for /ʧ/ or refer to the therapeutic tips for /ʃ/ in Chapter 7. The production technique and sound may not be perfect; however, practice the approximated sound and it should improve with practice.

Evaluation Outcome #2:

/ʧ/ & /ʤ/ are misarticulated

If the student misproduces /ʧ/ and /ʤ/, but can correctly produce /ʃ/ and /ʒ/ use the methods below to begin treatment. Review the section on "Tips for Transferring Successful Elicitation from One Word Position to Another" (page 21) and the "Therapeutic Tips for CH" in Chapter 5 for more information.

I. Elicitation Technique for /ʧ/.

These techniques and exercises will aid in elicitation and production of /ʧ/.

/t/ Final + /j/ Initial ⇨ /ʧ/ Medial
Example: get + you ⇨ getchew

Use the /t/ Final + /j/ Initial combination technique as discussed on page 25. Use the worksheets and exercises found on page 59.

/t/ Final + /ʃ/ Initial ⇨ /ʧ/ Medial
*Example: Night +**sh**ade ⇨ nigh**tch**ade*

When produced in rapid succession, /t/ final and /ʃ/ initial creates a /ʧ/ medial word, because the /ʧ/ naturally combines the "stop" trait of the /t/ with the continuant nature of the /ʃ/. Use the worksheets on pages 61-62 for phrase and sentence practice. When the student has mastered these exercises, progress to medial /ʃ/ single words. Review as necessary.

/n/ Final + /ʃ/ Initial ⇨ /ʧ/ Medial
*Example: te**n** + **sh**ips ⇨ te**nch**ips*

Production of the phoneme /n/ requires the tongue tip to approximate the alveolar ridge region. This leaves the tongue in the approximate production zone of the /ʧ/ stop position. Therefore, it provides an excellent starting point and makes production of /ʧ/ easier. Use the worksheets "N Final + SH Initial Elicitation Phrases and Sentences" on page 63-64.

After the student has mastered the combination of sounds, progress to medial /ʃ/ single words. Review as necessary.

II. Practice /ʧ/ medial single words, phrases, sentences, reading and carry-over activities.

The /ʧ/ medial position is most successfully elicited through the combinations above. Once /ʧ/ is attained through the use of elicitation techniques the instructor should progress to /ʧ/ medial single words. See "CH Medial Single Words" starting on page 79. Progress through phrases, sentences and carry-over activities. Once /ʧ/ medial is mastered move on to the /ʧ/ final word position.

III. Practice /ʧ/ final single words, phrases, sentences, reading and carry-over activities.

/n/ Medial + /ʧ/ Final ⇨ /ʧ/ Final

*Example: in**ch***

As in the /n/ final + /ʃ/ initial exercise on the previous page, use /n/ as a phonemic "elicitation point" to stimulate /ʧ/ in the final word position. Words with /n/ immediately prior to the /ʧ/ tend to be easier for students to produce. Use the worksheets found on page 65. Another technique to stimulate production of /ʧ/ final is to instruct the student to say the letter "H." Once success has been attained, progress to /ʧ/ final single words, phrases, sentences and carry-over activities. See "CH Final Single Words" starting on page 87.

IV. Save /ʧ/ initial words for last.

Remediating initial /ʧ/ words tends to be the most difficult because there are no approximate phonemic production zone assists. Some students, however, might find it easier since there are no preceding phonemes. Use the worksheets for /ʧ/ initial starting on page 71.

V. Remediating /ʤ/

The /ʤ/ is the voiced cognate of /ʧ/. Sometimes educating the student on the difference between a voiced sound (vocal cords turned on) and a voiceless sound (vocal cords turned off) is all that it takes. If that step doesn't work, try these techniques:

/d/ Final + /j/ Final ⇨ /ʤ/ Medial

Example: read + *your* ⇨ rea**dg**our

As discussed previously, and used in the exercises /s/ + /j/ and /t/ + /j/, the /j/ is a palatal semi-vowel that offers a good approximation point for /ʤ/. The main difference between /ʧ/ and /ʤ/ is the voicing aspect. The facilitating stop consonant for /ʤ/ is /d/ which is the voiced cognate for /t/. Hence, all of the exercises for /ʤ/ are similar to /ʧ/ only we substitute /d/ for /t/. Complete the "D Final + Y Initial" exercises found on pages 103-104. Once competence with /ʤ/ is achieved, progress to the next combination.

/d/ Final + /ʤ/ Final ⇨ /ʤ/ Final

Example: plaid + *jacket* ⇨ plai**dg**acket

This combination uses the final /d/ and initial /ʤ/ to approximate a /ʤ/ medial. Use the "D Final + J Initial" worksheets found on pages 105-107. The exercises increase in complexity from phrases to sentences with the /ʤ/ phrase in isolation. Once the student has placement of /ʤ/, use the next combination for reinforcement.

/ʤ/ Final + /ʤ/ Initial ⇨ /ʤ/ Initial

Example: village + *gypsy* ⇨ *gypsy*

This exercise uses production of /ʤ/ final to stabilize production in the initial word position. Instruct the student to say the word combination, pause, then say the word in isolation. Complete the worksheets found on pages 108-111.

VI. Practice /ʤ/ initial, medial, and final single words, phrases, sentences, reading and carry-over activities.

Use the worksheets beginning on page 113 for reinforcement and practice. Don't be constrained by the order of pages. If the medial position is more successful for the student, focus on that position first.

Evaluation Outcome #3:

/ʃ/ & /ʒ/ are misarticulated

If the student is misproducing /ʃ/ and /ʒ/, but can correctly produce /ʧ/ and /ʤ/, the following tips will assist in treatment. Review the section on "Tips for Transferring Successful Elicitation from One Word Position to Another" (page 21) and "Therapeutic Tips for SH" in Chapter 7.

I. Elicitation Techniques for /ʃ/:

First, elongate the /ʧ/ sound:

chshhhhhh

This simple exercise is sometimes all it takes to stimulate a correct /ʃ/ production. If it doesn't work, try this combination exercise to stimulate /ʃ/:

/ʧ/ Final + /ʃ/ Initial ⇨ /ʃ/ Medial

*Example: ea**ch** **sh**ark ⇨ ea**chsh**ark*

This exercise elaborates on the technique above by elongating the /ʧ/ sound. The final /ʧ/ and initial /ʃ/ are used to create an elongated /ʧ/: "eachshhhh shhhhhhark." Beginning on page 149, use the elicitation phrases, sentences and lastly the sentence pairs for practice. The sentence pairs offer two contexts of practice, one with phonemic approximation and one without. If this technique doesn't work, try this combination:

/s/ Final + /j/ Initial ⇨ /ʃ/ Medial

*Example: kis**s** **y**ou ⇨ kis**sh**oe*

Use the "S Final + Y Initial" worksheets found on page 146 to create /ʃ/ medial. After the student has mastered this combination, progress to /ʃ/ medial single words (starting on page 165). If the student continues to have difficulty with /ʃ/ medial words but can say /ʃ/ final words, this combination is very helpful:

/ʃ/ Final + /ʃ/ Initial ⇨ /ʃ/ Medial

Example: Spani__sh__ + __sh__ampoo ⇨ Spani__sh__ampoo

The word combinations in this exercise are designed to transfer a correct /ʃ/ final into a /ʃ/ medial word combination. The technique is to glide the final /ʃ/ into the initial, resulting in medial word production. Complete the exercises found on page 154. Instruct the student to say the phrase, pause then say the /ʃ/ initial word in isolation.

II. Practice /ʃ/ medial single words, phrases, sentences, reading and carry-over activities.

The medial position tends to be the easiest to produce, because it can be elicited through the combinations above. Therefore, more options are presented to stimulate production. Once correct production is attained through the elicitation techniques, the instructor should introduce "SH Medial Single Words" starting on page 165. Progress through phrases, sentences and carry-over activities. Once /ʃ/ medial is mastered move on to /ʃ/ final words.

III. Practice /ʃ/ initial and final single words, phrases, sentences, reading and carry-over activities.

Once the phoneme is stabilized, practice the sounds using the worksheets starting on page 157, for reinforcement and practice. Don't be constrained by the order in which the worksheets appear. If one position is more successful for the student, focus on that position first.

IV. Remediating /ʒ/.

The phoneme /ʒ/ is the least used consonant in the English language. The number of words that incorporate this sound are limited and many words are advanced. Thus, training options are limited. There are no approximate phonemic production assist exercise worksheets included for /ʒ/. The best method for eliciting /ʒ/ is to obtain /ʃ/ and then explain to the student that /ʒ/ is really /ʃ/ with the vocal cords "turned on." Provide both ear and vocal training for /ʒ/. Use the worksheets, starting on page 187 for /ʒ/ medial and final words practice.

Tips to Elicit /ʃ/, /ʧ/, /ʒ/ and /ʤ/

Instructing your student(s) to correctly produce a /ʃ/, /ʒ/, /ʧ/ or /ʤ/ is the first and sometimes most frustrating task. Fortunately, there are a number of techniques that can assist in your remediation efforts. For phoneme specific tricks, see the information in each chapter.

➢ Use a **mirror** as a visual cue for the student to see whether or not his tongue and lips are correctly positioned. Encourage the student to use the mirror. Show him that he shouldn't be able to see his tongue tip if his tongue is in the correct spot. Model the sound for your student and instruct him to use the mirror to imitate your actions. Inform the student that the tongue should be positioned behind the front top teeth toward the palato-alveolar region. Use the mirror to demonstrate where this region is located. Allow the student time to get acquainted with the specific parts of his mouth. Repeat this exercise as needed in each session until the student is able to kinesthetically "feel" where his tongue needs to be positioned.

➢ Another mirror technique is to practice lip movement. For all the sounds, the lips need to protrude slightly. It's not necessary to over-exaggerate lip protrusion. The mirror will allow the student to see how much extension is necessary. Practice lip movement by going from an /s/ to /ʃ/ and then /ʃ/ back to /s/. Repeat as necessary.

➢ **Draw out a big SH or CH** and have the student trace it. This is a tactile and visual cue that aids in focusing the student's attention on better production (see Big CH and SH activities on pages 55 and 144).

➢ If the student can say a /ʒ/ or /ʤ/, try to devoice the sounds to obtain a /ʃ/ or /ʧ/. Likewise, if the student can produce /ʃ/ and /ʧ/, but not /ʒ/ and /ʤ/, try voicing the sounds.

➢ If the student has one sound but not the others, practice training his ears to discriminate the differences in sounds. Perform contrast exercises, such as /ʧ/ versus /ʃ/, /ʧ/ versus /ʤ/, or /ʃ/ versus /ʒ/.

➢ After attaining success, **tape record** the student's correct productions from the combination sounds. Re-play the tape to the student to show him that he can produce the sound. It will also aid in performing the sounds in isolation.

➢ Perform ear training (or phonemic awareness) exercises. Read stories or word lists, so that the student can hear the repetition of the target phonemes. This will train him to listen to the subtle differences in the sound.

➢ Minimize group size. It may be necessary when first remediating to see the student individually or in a smaller group setting to achieve placement and gain confidence.

➢ If the student can produce a correct /s/ sound, instruct him to say /ʃ/, by bringing his tongue backward toward the hard palate.

➢ To **demonstrate forward airflow** the clinician can place a feather, a piece of paper, or a tissue in front of the student's mouth. The feather should be noticeably blown forward when a correct /ʃ/ or /ʧ/ is produced. Instruct the student to close his teeth into a natural bite, as if chewing, and then exhale. A correct /ʃ/ or /ʧ/ results in the air flowing straight out of the mouth.

➢ For a lateral /s/ disorder or nasal emission, a feather, paper or tissue is an excellent visual cue to promote awareness of proper airflow. If the /s/ and /ʃ/ production is lateralized, then the airflow will be on the sides and the feather or paper will move only on the sides of the mouth. For nasal emission use the same technique only isolate nasal flow. A mirror also works well to show moisture.

➢ Instruct the student to **elongate the /θ/ sound** (th). As he gradually pulls the tongue in and slides the tongue tip up on the backside of the upper front teeth to the alveolar ridge region, the /s/ sound should result. Continue to retract the tongue until /ʃ/ emerges. This exercise is not recommended for students with a frontal lisp disorder.

➢ For all exercises, ensure that the student **maintains a natural bite** when producing his sounds. Encourage good habits when the mouth is in a resting position. This will increase carryover that will be mantained in conversational speech.

➢ Good charting will provide you with the best record and measure of progress. Keeping good notes will make therapy much easier. Not only will you have you an excellent idea of where to begin from session to session, but you'll have a history of student performance.

➢ Send home homework only when the student is sufficiently competent with a sound. I recommend sound stabilization with at least 80% mastery over the course of a minimum of five sessions. To reinforce good habits, send home homework one to two levels below what the student is capable of achieving in the therapy session. For example, if the student is 80% accurate at the phrase level, send home single words for homework practice.

Student Practice Book

Incorporate as many modalities as possible into your therapy sessions to accelerate remediation. Using visual, auditory, and tactile exercises will add to increased learning.

A very useful tool is to instruct your students to make a "book" of their target sound (or sounds). Encourage the student to color pictures, make sentences, and create a story centered around words and sounds that are being targeted.

Students love the interactive nature of creating a book of their own. Encourage him to say the target words aloud as often as appropriate. Ask your students questions to engage them in structured conversational activities.

The single word and phrase worksheets found throughout this book are all formatted with a dotted template. Photocopy the pages and instruct the student to cut out the appropriate squares along the dotted lines. Color in the pictures as appropriate. Arrange the order of the pages and staple together. Figure 3-3 shows a sample story. Alternately, use the cut out squares as flash cards for drilling or for games such as "memory."

A blank template that matches the single words and phrases is provided on the opposite page. Use this for free hand drawing or for inserting text for story telling.

Figure 3-3 *Sample story*

Practice Book Template

CHAPTER 4: Case Studies

Case Studies

The case study worksheets in this chapter are designed for speech-language pathologists as a guide to evaluate and treat students using ***The Entire World of SH & CH***™ program.

Use these examples as a reference to interpret evaluation results, write specific goals and objectives, and to develop an effective easy-to-use remediation strategy.

Most importantly, by seeing how the evaluation and treatment process works, you will gain a greater appreciation of how this workbook and ***The Entire World of SH & CH***™ approach can accelerate your therapy.

Case Study #1
/ʃ/ and /ʒ/

Background:

Sharon Miller is a five year-old kindergartner at Carrillo Elementary School. Due to articulation errors, her classroom teacher referred Sharon to the speech-language pathologist. You complete a comprehensive screening using ***The Entire World of SH & CH™ Screening Form.***

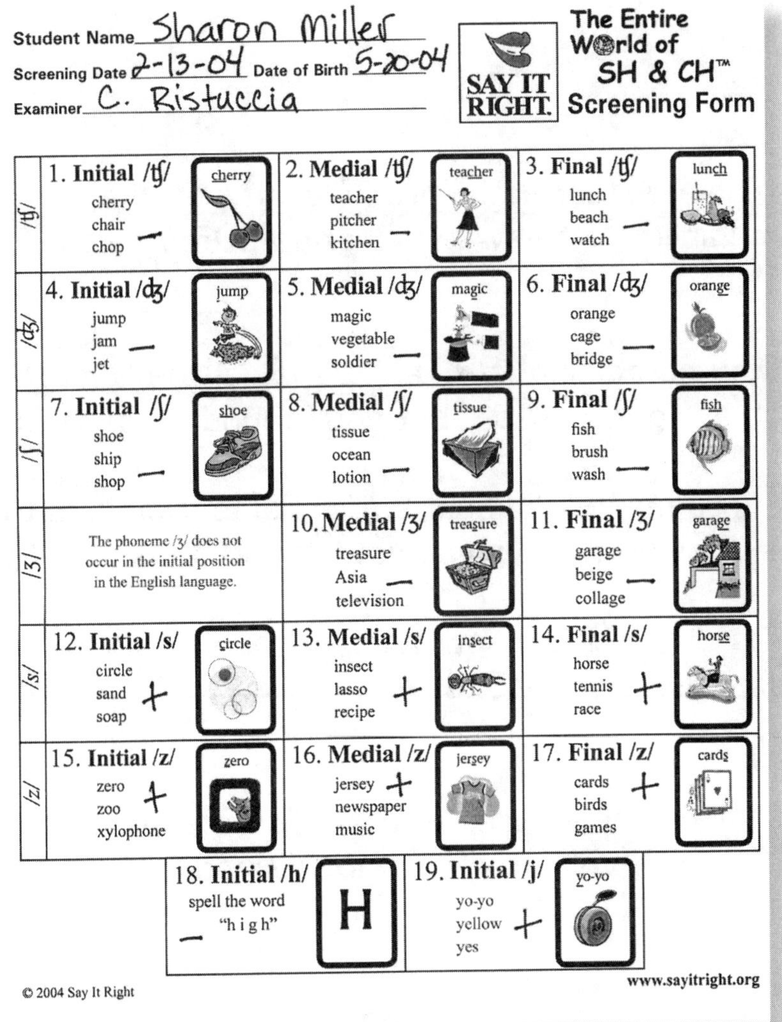

Student Name Sharon Miller
Screening Date 2-13-04 Date of Birth 5-20-04
Examiner C. Ristuccia

SAY IT RIGHT
The Entire World of SH & CH™ Screening Form

/tʃ/	1. Initial /tʃ/ cherry, chair, chop – (cherry)	2. Medial /tʃ/ teacher, pitcher, kitchen – (teacher)	3. Final /tʃ/ lunch, beach, watch – (lunch)
/dʒ/	4. Initial /dʒ/ jump, jam, jet – (jump)	5. Medial /dʒ/ magic, vegetable, soldier – (magic)	6. Final /dʒ/ orange, cage, bridge – (orange)
/ʃ/	7. Initial /ʃ/ shoe, ship, shop – (shoe)	8. Medial /ʃ/ tissue, ocean, lotion – (tissue)	9. Final /ʃ/ fish, brush, wash – (fish)
/ʒ/	The phoneme /ʒ/ does not occur in the initial position in the English language.	10. Medial /ʒ/ treasure, Asia, television – (treasure)	11. Final /ʒ/ garage, beige, collage – (garage)
/s/	12. Initial /s/ circle, sand, soap + (circle)	13. Medial /s/ insect, lasso, recipe + (insect)	14. Final /s/ horse, tennis, race + (horse)
/z/	15. Initial /z/ zero, zoo, xylophone + (zero)	16. Medial /z/ jersey, newspaper, music + (jersey)	17. Final /z/ cards, birds, games + (cards)
	18. Initial /h/ spell the word "h i g h" – (H)	19. Initial /j/ yo-yo, yellow, yes + (yo-yo)	

© 2004 Say It Right www.sayitright.org

Figure 4-1
Sharon Miller's screening results

Evaluation Summary:

As shown by her screening results (Figure 4-1), Sharon misarticulates /ʃ/, /ʒ/, /ʧ/ and /ʤ/.

Sample Goals and Objectives:

• Sharon will produce the /ʃ/ and /ʒ/ phonemes with 80% accuracy as related to core curriculum as measured by therapist tally and probe tests in single words, phrases and sentences.

• Sharon will produce the /ʧ/ and /ʤ/ phonemes with 80% accuracy as related to core curriculum as measured by therapist tally and probe tests in reading aloud, structured and spontaneous conversation.

Remediation Plan:

1). Since Sharon was not able to correctly produce any of the target sounds, probe further for stimulability. Review "Evaluation Outcome #1" on page 25.

2). Test stimulability for /ʧ/ by combining /t/ final + /j/ initial to elicit /ʧ/ in the medial word position, such as "ge**t** **y**ou" or "be**t** **y**ou" found on page 59.

3). Test stimulability for /ʃ/ by combining /s/ final + /j/ initial to elicit /ʃ/ in the medial word position, such as "kis**s** **y**ou" or "pla**ce** **y**ou" found on page 146.

Probing determines that Sharon is most stimulable for /ʃ/ since her pronunciation of "kiss you" sounds very close to /ʃ/. Proceed to "Evaluation Outcome #3" on page 31.

4). Continue with /s/ final + /j/ initial phrases and sentence exercises on pages 146-148. Skip the exercises involving /ʧ/ for now, since Sharon was not as stimulable for /ʧ/.

5). With some competence attained in the medial position, try "SH Medial Single Words, Phrases and Sentences" starting on page 165. Continue with reading aloud and carry-over activities.

6). Once the student is able to produce /ʃ/ in the medial position, try /ʃ/ final + /ʃ/ initial combinations. Do the exercise on page 154. Begin by instructing the student to pronounce the /ʃ/ medial word (e.g. Spani**sh**ampoo). Slow down production and pause to separate the two words: Spani**shhh** <*pause*> **sh**ampoo.

7). Complete /ʃ/ final + /ʃ/ initial phrases with isolation (e.g. The bru**sh** **sh**op. ⇨ **sh**op) and sentence pairs exercises (e.g. We use Spani**sh** **sh**ampoo and **Sh**ampoo that is Spani**sh** works the best) on pages 154-156.

8). Practice /ʃ/ final and initial single words, phrases and sentences. Continue with reading aloud, carry-over and structured conversational activities.

9). With competence attained with /ʃ/, work on the voiced cognate /ʒ/. Review with the student the differences in voiced and voiceless speech. Instruct the student to "turn on" her voice box for /ʒ/. Since exposure to /ʒ/ may be limited (due to the limited number of vocabulary words available), perform phonemic awareness training by reading aloud practice words or reading a story from ***The Entire World of SH & CH™ Book of Stories***. Practice /ʒ/ medial and final single words, phrases and sentences starting with "ZH Medial Single Words" found on page 187.

10). Once /ʃ/ is successfully mastered in all positions, attempt to treat /ʧ/ and /ʤ/ by following the recommended techniques in Evaluation Outcome #2 on page 28.

Case Study #2 Treating /ʧ/ When the Student Can Say /ʃ/

Background:

Mary Marshall is a 5 year-old kindergartner at Bobier Elementary School. Her classroom teacher referred Mary to the speech-language pathologist due to her misproductions of /ʧ/ words. You do a comprehensive screening utilizing ***The Entire World of SH & CH™ Screening Form.***

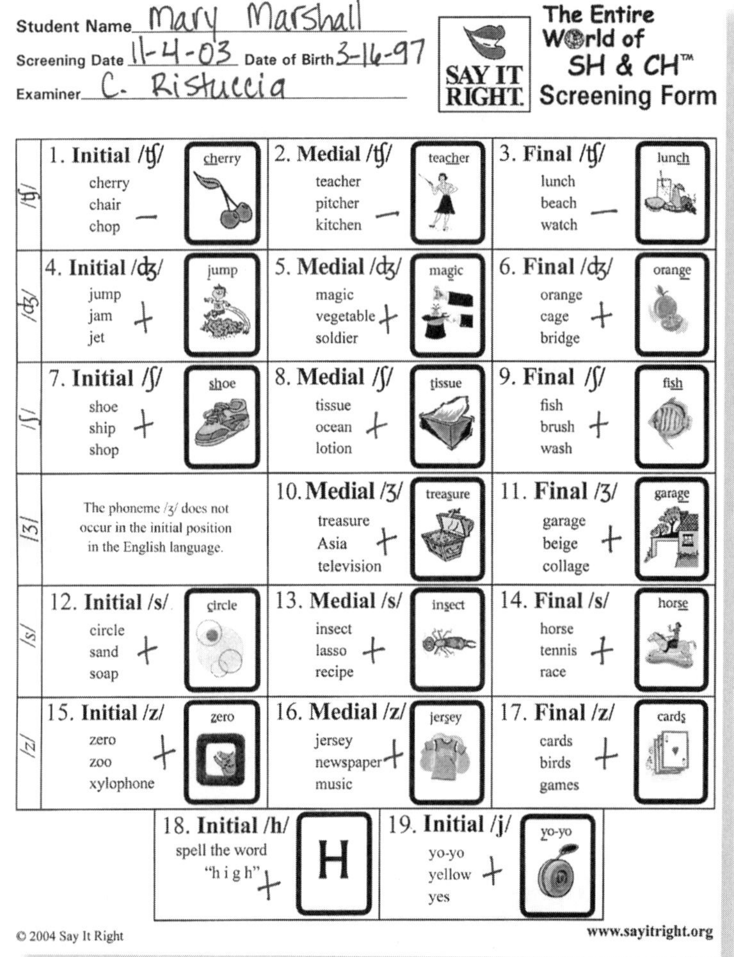

Student Name Mary Marshall
Screening Date 11-4-03 Date of Birth 3-16-97
Examiner C. Ristuccia

SAY IT RIGHT — The Entire World of SH & CH™ Screening Form

/ʧ/	1. Initial /ʧ/ cherry, chair, chop — (cherry)	2. Medial /ʧ/ teacher, pitcher, kitchen — (teacher)	3. Final /ʧ/ lunch, beach, watch — (lunch)
/ʤ/	4. Initial /ʤ/ jump, jam, jet + (jump)	5. Medial /ʤ/ magic, vegetable, soldier + (magic)	6. Final /ʤ/ orange, cage, bridge + (orange)
/ʃ/	7. Initial /ʃ/ shoe, ship, shop + (shoe)	8. Medial /ʃ/ tissue, ocean, lotion + (tissue)	9. Final /ʃ/ fish, brush, wash + (fish)
/ʒ/	The phoneme /ʒ/ does not occur in the initial position in the English language.	10. Medial /ʒ/ treasure, Asia, television + (treasure)	11. Final /ʒ/ garage, beige, collage + (garage)
/s/	12. Initial /s/ circle, sand, soap + (circle)	13. Medial /s/ insect, lasso, recipe + (insect)	14. Final /s/ horse, tennis, race + (horse)
/z/	15. Initial /z/ zero, zoo, xylophone + (zero)	16. Medial /z/ jersey, newspaper, music + (jersey)	17. Final /z/ cards, birds, games + (cards)
	18. Initial /h/ spell the word "h i g h" + (H)	19. Initial /j/ yo-yo, yellow, yes + (yo-yo)	

© 2004 Say It Right www.sayitright.org

Figure 4-2
Mary Marshall's screening results

Evaluation Summary:

Mary's screening results (Figure 4-2), indicate that she misproduces /ʧ/ in the initial, medial, and final word positions. However, she is able to successfully pronounce /ʃ/, /ʤ/ and /ʒ/ words.

Sample Goals and Objectives:

• Mary will produce the /ʧ/ phoneme with 80% accuracy over five consecutive therapy sessions as related to core curriculum as measured by therapist tally and probe tests in single words, phrases, and sentences.

Remediation Plan:

1). Since Mary is able to produce some of the sibilant sounds, we will use the sounds that she can produce to elicit misproduced phonemes.

2). Review "Evaluation Outcome #2" found on page 28.

3) Since /ʃ/ is correctly produced, use /t/ final + /ʃ/ initial words to elicit /ʧ/ in the medial word position (e.g. sof**t sh**ell or nigh**t sh**ade). Practice the "T Final + SH Initial" exercises on page 61.

4). Say "get you" rapidly as one word until a medial /ʧ/ is produced (e.g. ge**t y**ou = ge**ch**ew). Practice the similar "T Final + Y Initial" exercises found on pages 59-60.

5). Use /t/ final + /ʃ/ initial words to elicit /ʧ/ in the medial word position at the sentence level (e.g. I found a sof**t sh**ell). Practice the exercises found on page 62.

6). Use /n/ final + /ʃ/ Initial words ("te**n sh**ips") to approximate /ʧ/ medial words. Practice the "N Final + SH Initial" exercises found on page 63.

7). Now try /ʧ/ medial words, phrases and sentences starting with "CH Medial Single Words" found on page 79. Continue with reading, carry-over, and structured conversation activities.

8). Review /n/ + /ʧ/ final words such as "i**nch** or "lu**nch**." Practice the exercises on page 65.

9). Use /ʧ/ final + /ʧ/ initial word combinations with initial /ʧ/ words in isolation (e.g. ea**ch** **ch**ild. ⇨ **ch**ild) and sentence pairs (e.g. Ea**ch** **ch**ild will bring a snack. The **ch**ildren will ea**ch** bring a snack.) to elicit /ʧ/ in the initial and final word positions. "CH Final + CH Initial" exercises are found on page 68.

10). Finally, try /ʧ/ initial and final words at the single word, phrase, and sentence levels starting with "CH Final Single Words" on page 71. Continue with reading, carry-over, and structured conversational activities.

11). Review the /ʤ/ exercises in Chapter 6 to ensure that the focus on /ʃ/ did not cause the student to devoice during production.

Case Study #3
/ʧ/ and /ʤ/

Background:

Chelsea Simon is a 6 year-old kindergartner at Islands Elementary School. Her classroom teacher is concerned with her speech and referred her to the speech-language pathologist. You complete a comprehensive screening using ***The Entire World of SH & CH™ Screening Form.***

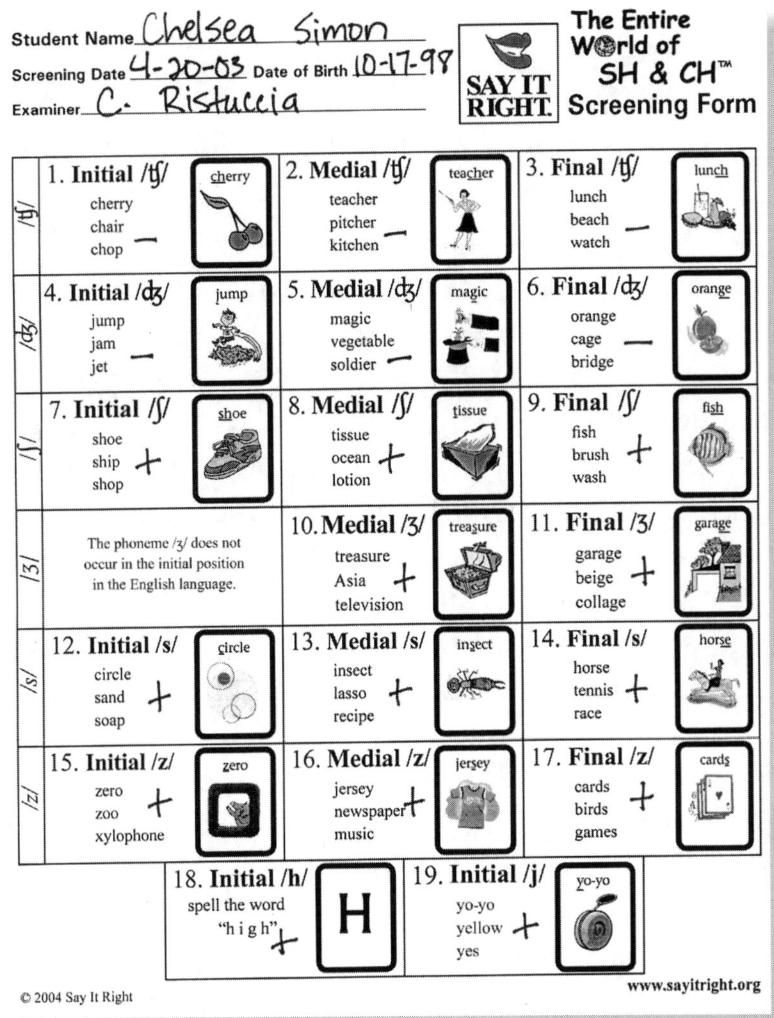

Student Name Chelsea Simon
Screening Date 4-20-03 Date of Birth 10-17-98
Examiner C. Ristuccia

SAY IT RIGHT.
The Entire World of SH & CH™ Screening Form

	Initial	Medial	Final
/ʧ/	1. Initial /ʧ/ cherry, chair, chop —	2. Medial /ʧ/ teacher, pitcher, kitchen —	3. Final /ʧ/ lunch, beach, watch —
/ʤ/	4. Initial /ʤ/ jump, jam, jet —	5. Medial /ʤ/ magic, vegetable, soldier —	6. Final /ʤ/ orange, cage, bridge —
/ʃ/	7. Initial /ʃ/ shoe, ship, shop +	8. Medial /ʃ/ tissue, ocean, lotion +	9. Final /ʃ/ fish, brush, wash +
/ʒ/	The phoneme /ʒ/ does not occur in the initial position in the English language.	10. Medial /ʒ/ treasure, Asia, television +	11. Final /ʒ/ garage, beige, collage +
/s/	12. Initial /s/ circle, sand, soap +	13. Medial /s/ insect, lasso, recipe +	14. Final /s/ horse, tennis, race +
/z/	15. Initial /z/ zero, zoo, xylophone +	16. Medial /z/ jersey, newspaper, music +	17. Final /z/ cards, birds, games +

18. Initial /h/	19. Initial /j/
spell the word "h i g h" +	yo-yo, yellow, yes +

© 2004 Say It Right www.sayitright.org

Figure 4-3
Chelsea Simon's screening results

Evaluation Summary:

As shown by her screening results (Figure 4-3), Chelsea misproduces /ʧ/ and /ʤ/. The phonemes /ʃ/ and /ʒ/ are producible. However, she correctly says the letter "H," which we can use to elicit /ʧ/ final.

Sample Goals and Objectives:

• Chelsea will produce the /ʧ/ and /ʤ/ phonemes with 80% accuracy as related to core curriculum as measured by therapist tally and probe tests in reading aloud, structured, and spontaneous conversation.

Remediation Plan:

1). Review Evaluation Outcome #2 on page 28.

2). Say "get you" rapidly as one word until a medial /ʧ/ is produced. (e.g. ge**t** **y**ou = ge**ch**ew).

3) Practice the similar /t/ final + /j/ initial phrase and sentence exercises starting with "T Final + Y Initial Elicitation Phrases" on page 59.

4) Since /ʃ/ is correctly produced, use /t/ final + /ʃ/ initial words to elicit /ʧ/ in the medial word position (e.g. sof**t** **sh**ell or nigh**t** **sh**ade). Practice the "T Final + SH Initial Elicitation Phrases" exercise found on page 61.

5). Use /t/ final + /ʃ/ initial words to elicit /ʧ/ in the medial word position at the sentence level (e.g. I found a sof**t** **sh**ell). Practice "T Final + SH Initial Elicitation Sentences" exercise found on page 62.

6). Use /n/ final + /ʃ/ initial words to approximate /ʧ/ medial words. Practice the exercises on page 63-64. Use /n/ final + /ʃ/ initial words to approximate /ʧ/ medial words.

7). Now try /ʧ/ medial words, phrases, and sentences starting with "CH Medial Single Words" on page 79. Continue with reading, carry-over, and structured conversational activities.

8). Since Chelsea is able to produce the letter "H," instruct her to say the letter "H." Repeat it several times. Practice /ʧ/ final words. Use the worksheets from "CH Final Single Words" found on page 87. Direct her to say "H" and then the word (e.g. H, ben**ch**; H, lun**ch**; H, por**ch**; etc.).

9). Review /n/ + /ʧ/ final words such as "i**nch** or "lu**nch**." Practice the exercises found on page 65.

10). Continue with /ʧ/ final reading, carry-over, and structured conversational activities.

11). Use /ʧ/ final + /ʧ/ initial word combinations with the initial /ʧ/ word in isolation (e.g. ea**ch** **ch**ild. ⇨ **ch**ild) and sentence pairs (e.g. Ea**ch** **ch**ild will bring a snack and The **ch**ildren will ea**ch** bring a snack.) to elicit /ʧ/ in initial and final word positions.

12). Finally, try /ʧ/ initial words at the single word, phrase, and sentence levels starting with the "CH Initial Single Words" found on page 71. Continue with reading, carry-over, and structured conversational activities.

13). Next review /ʤ/ exercises found in Chapter 6. The /ʤ/ phoneme is the voiced cognate of /ʧ/. Review the differences in voiced and voiceless speech. Instruct the student to "turn on" her voice-box for /ʤ/.

14). Use /d/ final + /j/ final word combinations (e.g. rea**d** **y**our or sen**d** **y**ou). Practice the "D Final + Y Initial Elicitation Phrases and Sentences" exercises starting on page 103.

15). Try /d/ final + /ʤ/ initial word combinations to elicit /ʤ/ in the medial position (e.g. plai**d** **j**acket or mixe**d** **j**am). Practice the "D Final + J Initial" exercises found on pages 105-107.

16). Finally, use /ʤ/ final + /ʤ/ initial words to stabilize production in the initial position by isolating the /ʤ/ initial word (e.g. villa**ge** **g**ypsy ⇨ **g**ypsy). Practice "J Final + J Initial" exercises starting on page 108.

CHAPTER 5:

The Entire World™ of...

Initial, Medial & Final

CH Teaching Tool

The /t͡ʃ/ or ch phoneme is a combination of the phonemes /t/ and sh. It is referred to as an *affricate,* because the sound is produced as a result of forcing air through a narrow opening in the mouth after the sound is initiated as a result of stopping the airflow.

The sound is created by the tongue tip touching the palato-alveolar region. The tongue can actually make contact from the upper central incisors back to the hard palate area. The important part is that the tongue must be firmly in place to cease the flow of air. To initiate the sound, the tongue tip is lowered quickly, releasing the airflow. The lateral portions of the tongue should be pressed against the upper back teeth forcing the airflow over the tongue.

The lips are protruded (pushed out) slightly and the corners of the mouth are also tensed.

The vocal cords do not vibrate when the ch phoneme is made.

Explain to the student that the sound ch is a combination of /t/ and sh and that she will be practicing isolating the two sounds, first /t/, then sh. Then slowly bring the two sounds together and repeat more rapidly until the sound is correct.

Use the exercises in this chapter to obtain successful production. First, the most basic exercise uses the /t/ final + y initial to elicit ch medial words (e.g. bet you ⇨ be**tch**u). Then, /t/ initial + sh initial is used to elicit ch medial. This is followed by /n/ final + sh initial and /n/ medial + ch final exercises.

Finally, starting on page 71, there are worksheets for ch in the initial, medial, and final word positions.

Figure 5-1 *"CH" visual cue*

Therapeutic Tips for CH

Involve as many senses as possible when teaching a student to correct an articulation/phonological disorder. Different modalities all contribute to a successful learning situation. Visual and tactile stimuli reinforce and complement auditory cueing techniques.

The following are a few ideas to try with your students. We encourage you to develop some of your own. Most importantly, use all of the tips simultaneously for maximum impact.

Auditory Tips

Refer to the ch as the "exploded chin sound." As the student touches her chin, the ch explodes. This auditory cue uses sound associations to learn new information.

Additionally, you can use the "choo choo" train sound or the sneezing sound (e.g."achoo" as though she is sneezing).

Practice the advanced auditory contrast exercise: *th, s, sh, ch.* Instruct the student to say this combination repeatedly in one breath. Speed-up production as fast as possible making sure the sounds are distinct. This exercise moves the tongue in sequence from front to back.

Incorporate ear training into your therapy. Read the target words or stories with the target words to the student. Instruct the student to raise her hand to identify the target sound when she hears it. Since the student is having difficulty producing the correct sound, the goal is to get her used to hearing the sound produced correctly.

Visual Tips

Make a copy of the large "CH" on page 55. Place this cue in front of the student at every session as a visual reference.

As an alternative strategy to the "exploded sound", touch your chin with your index finger and push it away from the face as you say the "ch" sound. See figure 5-1.

Another visual cue is to extend your hand out as though you are showing all five fingers as you make the "ch" sound. Emphasize the explosive nature of ch. See Figure 6-2 and 6-3 on page 99.

Instruct your students to remember the "exploded chin sound" when producing ch. Perform this cue for students when they are first learning how to produce the ch, and as reinforcement later when your students are having difficulty with the sound.

Tactile Tips

Tactile or kinesthetic cues use the student's sense of touch to learn information. Model the ch sound for the student. The mouth should be slightly open with the teeth showing. Point an index finger to the chin. As you make the ch, move your finger away from your chin with a quick motion simultaneously as you explode the ch sound. Instruct the student to use this cue to develop kinesthetic awareness of proper tongue positioning and air flow.

Another tactile cue is to instruct the student to color in the letters on the ch worksheets found on page 56. The process of coloring focuses the student on the ch sound.

Use a mirror so the student can see proper mouth and lip positioning. Model the sound for the student.

For initial, medial and final single word and phrase worksheets, instruct the student to color in the pictures. Also, cut out the pictures and arrange them into a booklet or use as flash cards for games and memory exercises. See page 36.

Remediation Tricks

1. Instructing the student to produce a quick, tight sh is sometimes effective in producing ch.

2. If the student is not explosively releasing airflow, it's probably due to the airway being blocked by the tongue. Try placing a feather or piece of paper in front of the student's mouth to give a visual indication of air flowing in a forward direction.

3. If the student's tongue is protruding so that the voiceless th is substituted for sh or if airflow is leaking laterally, then the student has a frontal/lateral lisp disorder. Use a mirror to demonstrate proper mouth and tongue positioning. Review the tips and techniques for frontal and lateral lisp disorders in ***The Entire World of S & Z™ Instructional Workbook.***

4. If the student is emitting sounds through the nose, bring this to her attention. Use a mirror or feather under the nose to show moisture or movement.

Big CH

Name: Date:

Directions: Color in the big "CH." This activity provides tactile and visual stimulation when producing the ch sound.

CH Activity: Ch-Ch-Ch-Cha

Name: Date:

Directions: Instructor should make up a word list. Instruct the student to pronounce the ch words. If correct, the student gets to color in a "CH." If incorrect, the instructor colors in a "CH." Continue until all the letters are colored.

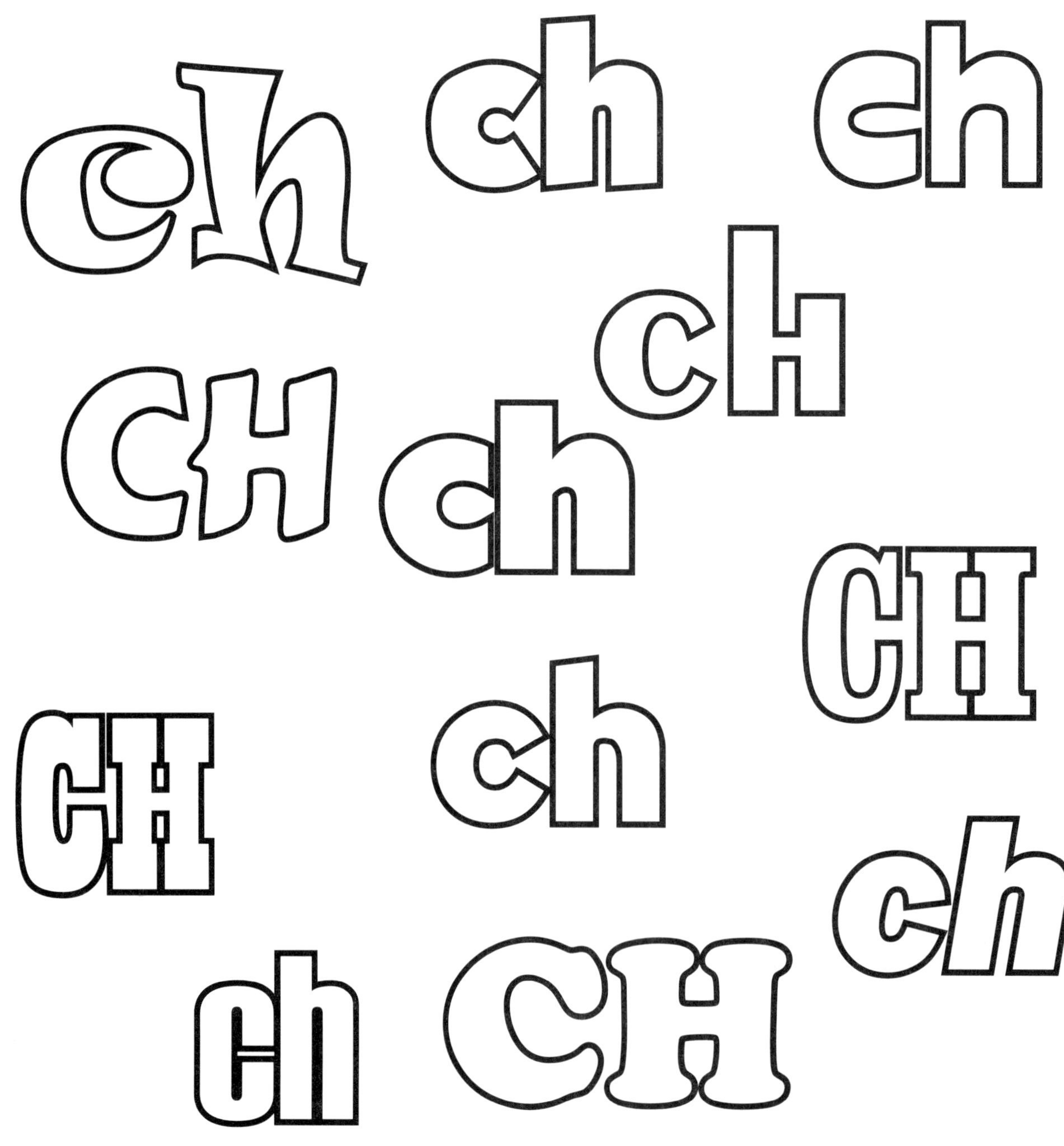

Choo Choo

Name: Date:

Directions: Color in the "choo choo" train. Make the "choo choo" sound while coloring. This activity provides tactile, auditory and visual stimulation when producing the ch sound.

CH Activity: Cheese

Name: Date:

Directions: Color in the cheese. Fill in the blank with the name of your favorite cheese. Do you know the name of a cheese that starts with "ch"?

My favorite cheese is____________________

T Final + Y Initial

Elicitation Phrases

Name: Date:

Directions: Use this exercise if the student cannot produce a ch. Say each sentence slowly. The t final + y initial combination creates a ch medial. Mark the speech/homework block as appropriate for correct pronunciation.

	Speech	Homework
1). Doubt you.	______	______
2). Bet you.	______	______
3). Get yellow paper.	______	______
4). I met you.	______	______
5). Ran past you.	______	______
6). Come and get you.	______	______
7). They fit you.	______	______
8). Light yellow light.	______	______
9). Let yellow bugs.	______	______
10). Beat you at tennis.	______	______
11). Cast you out to sea.	______	______
12). Sent yellow flowers.	______	______

T Final + Y Initial

Elicitation Sentences with CH Initial in Isolation

Name: Date:

Directions: Use this exercise for production of ch initial by using a t final and y initial combination. Say each sentence slowly; pause and pronounce the ch initial word in isolation. Emphasis is on a clear ch. Mark the speech/homework block as appropriate for correct pronunciation.

	Speech	Homework
1). We doubt your story. ⇨ chore	______	______
2). I will bet you five cents. ⇨ chew	______	______
3). Please get yellow paper. ⇨ chello	______	______
4). Bob will greet you at a party. ⇨ chew	______	______
5). Mary ran right past you. ⇨ chew	______	______
6). Come and get your snack. ⇨ chore	______	______
7). The pants fit you well.⇨ chew	______	______
8). Light yellow lights for dinner. ⇨chello	______	______
9). Jim sent yellow flowers.⇨ chello	______	______
10). Mary can beat you at tennis. ⇨ chew	______	______
11). Carol bought you some flowers.⇨chew	______	______
12). It is fun to let yellow bugs land on you. ⇨ chew	______	______

T Final + SH Initial

Elicitation Phrases to Produce CH Medial

Name: Date:

Directions: Use this exercise to obtain production of ch medial. Say each phrase slowly; then repeat and speed up production. Mark the speech/homework block as appropriate for correct pronunciation.

	Speech	Homework
1). Bright shell.	______	______
2). Night shade.	______	______
3). Cut short hair.	______	______
4). Nut shell.	______	______
5). Bent shovel.	______	______
6). Coat shop.	______	______
7). Night shadow.	______	______
8). Eat shrimp.	______	______
9). Boat show.	______	______
10). Meet Shawn.	______	______
11). Mint shampoo.	______	______
12). Eat shortcake.	______	______

T Final + SH Initial
Elicitation Sentences

Name: Date:

Directions: Use this exercise to obtain production of ch medial. Say each sentence slowly; then repeat and speed up production. Mark the speech/homework block as appropriate for correct pronunciation.

	Speech	Homework
1). The snail has a sof**t** **sh**ell.	______	______
2). We sat under the nigh**t** **sh**ade.	______	______
3). Bill likes to cu**t** **sh**ort hair.	______	______
4). David dropped the nu**t** **sh**ell.	______	______
5). Carol tried to use the ben**t** **sh**ovel.	______	______
6). Matt went to the coa**t** **sh**op.	______	______
7). The nigh**t** **sh**adows were scary.	______	______
8). For dinner we will ea**t** **sh**rimp and pasta.	______	______
9). Leslie set up for the boa**t** **sh**ow.	______	______
10). Ann likes to ea**t** **sh**ortcake.	______	______
11). I like to use peppermin**t** **sh**ampoo.	______	______
12). We are going to mee**t** **Sh**awn and Jim at five o'clock.	______	______

N Final + SH Initial

Elicitation Phrases to Produce CH Medial

Name: Date:

Directions: This exercise used the approximate phonemic production of n + sh initial to obtain ch medial. Say each phrase slowly; then repeat and speed up production. Mark the speech/homework block as appropriate for correct pronunciation.

	Speech	Homework
1). Ten ships.	______	______
2). Ben shops.	______	______
3). Television show.	______	______
4). Rain shower.	______	______
5). Broken shoelace.	______	______
6). Forgotten shoe.	______	______
7). Fourteen sheep.	______	______
8). Pay attention Sherry!	______	______
9). Pawn shop.	______	______
10). Broken shell.	______	______
11). Cotton sheets.	______	______
12). In the sun shine.	______	______

N Final + SH Initial
Elicitation Sentences

Name: Date:

Directions: Say each sentence slowly; then repeat up production. Mark the speech/ homework block as appropriate for correct pronunciation.

	Speech	Homework
1). We saw te**n** **sh**ips.	______	______
2). Be**n** **sh**ops at the store down the street.	______	______
3). The televisio**n** **sh**ow is on at 8:00 pm.	______	______
4). There was a rai**n** **sh**ower today.	______	______
5). Colleen has a broke**n** **sh**oelace.	______	______
6). Sue is outside in the su**n** **sh**ine.	______	______
7). Fourtee**n** **sh**eep were in the yard.	______	______
8). Pay attentio**n** **Sh**erry!	______	______
9). We sold the ring to the paw**n** **sh**op.	______	______
10). Ben found a broke**n** **sh**ell.	______	______
11). Clea**n** **sh**eets were put on the bed.	______	______
12). We found a forgotte**n** **sh**oe.	______	______

N + CH Activity: Quilting Bee

Name: Date:

Directions: Find the words that end with the letters "***nch***." Say the word aloud and color in that triangle to make your quilt.

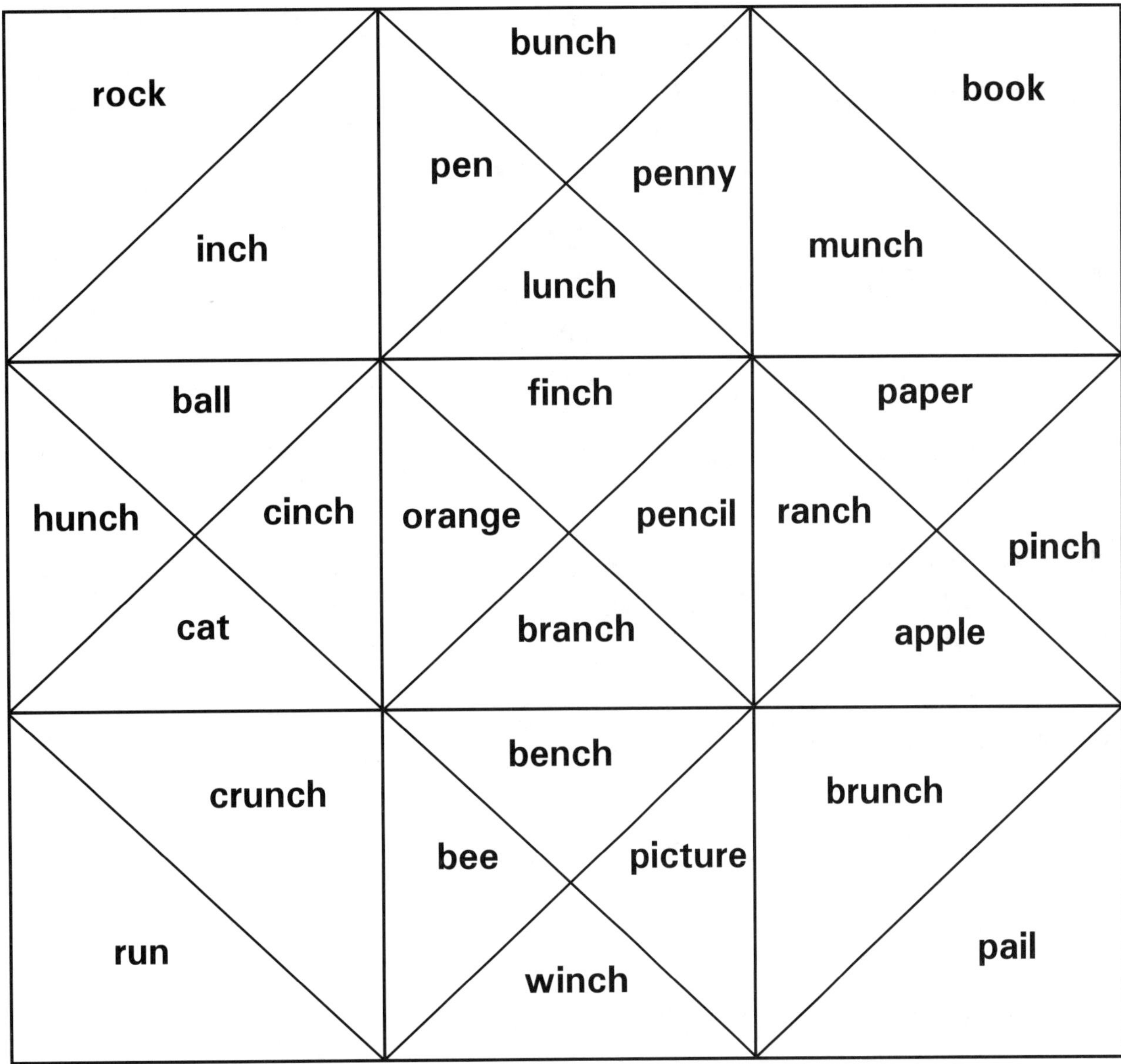

N Final + CH Initial Phrases

Name: Date:

Directions: Use this exercise to create ch medial words from n final + ch initial words. Say each phrase slowly with emphasis on combining the n final and ch initial words. Repeat with emphasis on separating the n final and ch words. Mark the speech/homework block as appropriate for correct pronunciation.

	Speech	Homework
1). Fourteen chairs.	______	______
2). Ten chips.	______	______
3). Broken chair.	______	______
4). Sun chair.	______	______
5). Fun cheer.	______	______
6). One cherry.	______	______
7). Tan chief.	______	______
8). Man chat.	______	______
9). Been chosen.	______	______
10). In China.	______	______
11). Run children.	______	______
12). Forgotten chimp.	______	______

N Final + CH Initial Sentences

Name: Date:

Directions: Use this exercise to create ch medial words from n final + ch initial words. Say each sentence slowly to combine the n final and ch initial words. Repeat with emphasis on separating the n final and ch initial words. Mark the speech/homework block as appropriate for correct pronunciation.

	Speech	Homework
1). There are fourteen chairs at the table.	_____	_____
2). We found ten chips in the bowl.	_____	_____
3). Do not sit on the broken chair.	_____	_____
4). The sun chair is in the backyard.	_____	_____
5). Let's hear your fun cheer.	_____	_____
6). Doug ate one cherry pie.	_____	_____
7). The tan chief stood tall.	_____	_____
8). The man chatted with the boy.	_____	_____
9). Lou had been chosen to go.	_____	_____
10). The toy was made in China.	_____	_____
11). Run children, run home!	_____	_____
12). The forgotten chimps are at the zoo.	_____	_____

CH Final + CH Initial

Using CH Final to Elicit CH Initial

Name: Date:

Directions: Use this exercise if the student can say ch in the final position, but not initial. Say each phrase slowly elongating the ch final into the ch initial making a ch medial word, pause and then say the ch initial word in isolation. Mark the speech/homework block as appropriate.

	Speech	Homework
1). Inch chew. ⇨ chew	______	______
2). Each child. ⇨ child	______	______
3). Beach chair. ⇨ chair	______	______
4). Lunch chore. ⇨ chore	______	______
5). Torch chimney. ⇨ chimney	______	______
6). Couch chair. ⇨ chair	______	______
7). Peach chocolate. ⇨ chocolate	______	______
8). Munch cheese. ⇨ cheese	______	______
9). Catch cherry. ⇨ cherry	______	______
10). Bench check. ⇨ check	______	______
11). Watch Charles. ⇨ Charles	______	______
12). Speech chair. ⇨ chair	______	______

CH Final + CH Initial

Sentence Pairs

Name: Date:

Directions: Say each sentence slowly. Cycle through each sentence pair. Elongate the ch final into the initial ch in the "A" sentence. Emphasize the ch initial in isolation for the "B" sentence.

	Speech/	Homework
1A). The dog will crun**ch**, **ch**ew and bite the bone.	____	____
1B). The dog will crun**ch**, bite and **ch**ew the bone.	____	____
2A). Ea**ch** **ch**ild will bring a snack.	____	____
2B). The **ch**ildren will ea**ch** bring a snack.	____	____
3A). Please bring the bea**ch** **ch**air.	____	____
3B). When you go to the bea**ch**, bring the **ch**air.	____	____
4A). Molly will do the lun**ch** **ch**ores.	____	____
4B). At lun**ch**, Molly will do the **ch**ores.	____	____
5A). The tor**ch** **ch**imney was black.	____	____
5B). The **ch**imney had a long tor**ch**.	____	____
6A). The spee**ch** **ch**air is where you sit during spee**ch**.	____	____
6B). Brenda sat in the **ch**air during spee**ch**.	____	____

CH Final + CH Initial
Sentence Pairs

Name: Date:

Directions: Say each sentence slowly. Cycle through each sentence pair. Elongate the ch final into the ch initial in the "A" sentence. Emphasize the ch initial in isolation for the "B" sentence.

	Speech/	Homework
7A). The cou**ch** **ch**air reclined.	____	____
7B). The cou**ch** also had a reclining **ch**air.	____	____
8A). The mice will mun**ch** **ch**eese for dinner.	____	____
8B). I saw the mouse mun**ch** on **ch**eese.	____	____
9A). Pea**ch** **ch**ocolate ice cream is my favorite.	____	____
9B). Mary liked the pea**ch** and **ch**ocolate for dessert.	____	____
10A). Cat**ch** **ch**erries falling from the tree.	____	____
10B). Under the tree, cat**ch** the falling **ch**erries.	____	____
11A). Wat**ch** **Ch**arles perform on stage.	____	____
11B). **Ch**arles performs while we wat**ch**.	____	____
12A). The ben**ch** **ch**ecked out O.K.	____	____
12B). When he **ch**ecked the ben**ch**, it was O.K.	____	____

CH Initial Single Words

Name: Date:

Directions: Say each word slowly. Make sure to elongate the initial ch sound. Mark the speech/homework block as appropriate for correct pronunciation.

chick

Speech ___ Homework ___

chair

Speech ___ Homework ___

cherry

Speech ___ Homework ___

cheese

Speech ___ Homework ___

chimp	chain

Speech ___ Homework ___	Speech ___ Homework ___
check	chin

Speech ___ Homework ___	Speech ___ Homework ___

More CH Initial Practice Words:

chore
charm
chump
champ

chicken
Charles
cheetah
Chauncy

CH Initial Phrases

Name: Date:

Directions: Say each phrase slowly. Make sure to elongate the initial ch sound. Mark the speech/homework block as appropriate for correct pronunciation.

See the <u>ch</u>icken.

Speech ___ Homework ___

Yummy, <u>ch</u>erry pie!

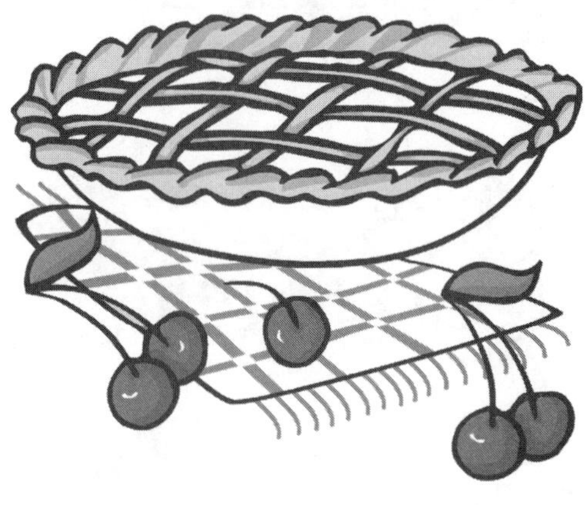

Speech ___ Homework ___

A fast <u>ch</u>eetah.

Speech ___ Homework ___

Tasty potato <u>ch</u>ips.

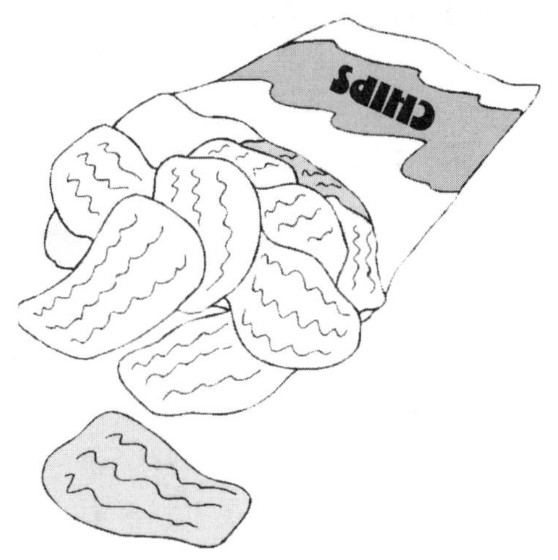

Speech ___ Homework ___

A brick chimney.

Speech ___ Homework ___

A choo choo train.

Speech ___ Homework ___

Four children.

Speech ___ Homework ___

A chicken egg.

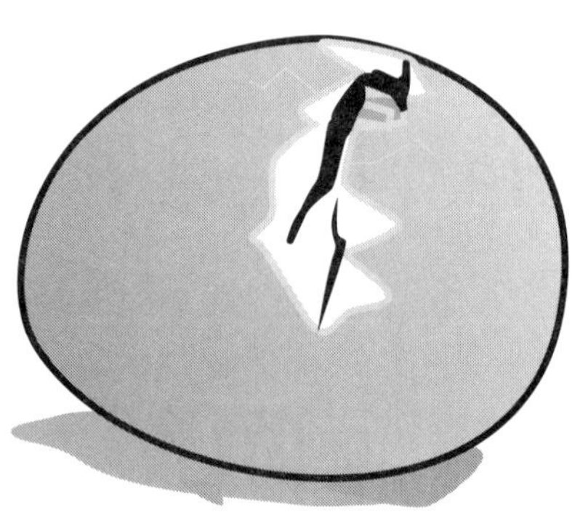

Speech ___ Homework ___

More CH Initial Practice Phrases:

Do your chores.
Some cheddar cheese.
A chocolate chip.
A chilly day.

Make a choice.
The chosen one.
A game of Chess.
Never cheat.

CH Initial Sentences

Name: Date:

Directions: Say each sentence slowly. Cycle through each set, changing the ending for a different ch target word. Mark the speech/homework block as appropriate for correct pronunciation.

Charlie chose...

Speech _ _ _ Homework _ _ _

the charms

the cherry

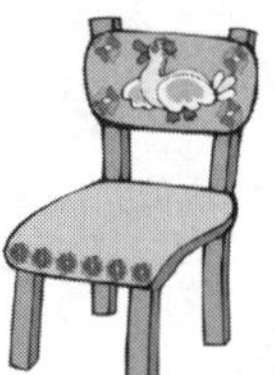

the chair

Chase likes the...

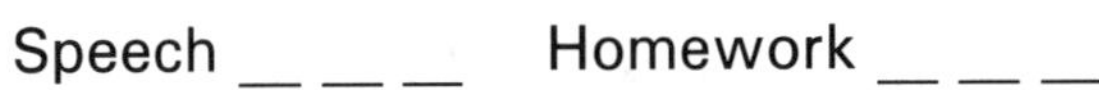

Speech _ _ _ Homework _ _ _

easy chore

champion

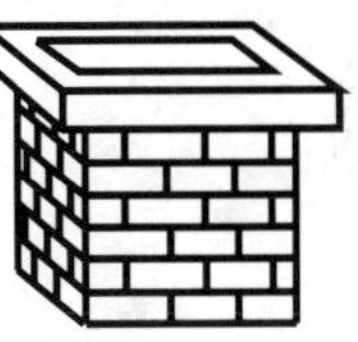

chimney

Speech _ _ _ Homework _ _ _

Chaz ate the...

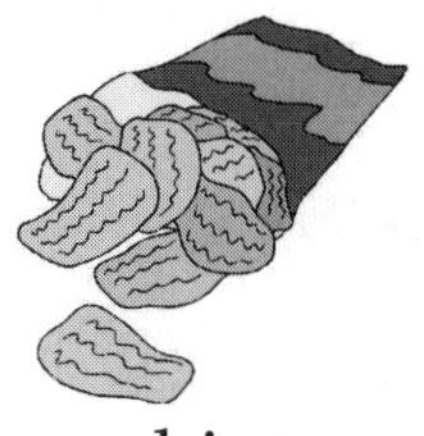

chips

chicken

cherry pie

Activity: Color In

Name: Date:

Directions: The instructor should make up a word list of ten words. Instruct the student to pronounce the words. For each correct answer, the student colors in a chick. For each incorrect answer, the instructor colors in a chick.

Activity: Cherry Tree

Name: Date:

Directions: The instructor should make up a word list of 12 words. Instruct the student to pronounce the words. For each correct answer, the student colors in a cherry. For each incorrect answer, the instructor colors in a cherry.

Activity: All Aboard!

Name: Date:

Directions: This train is making tracks. There are ten railroad ties that need to be filled in. Instruct the student to pronounce each word and color in a railroad tie for each correct answer.

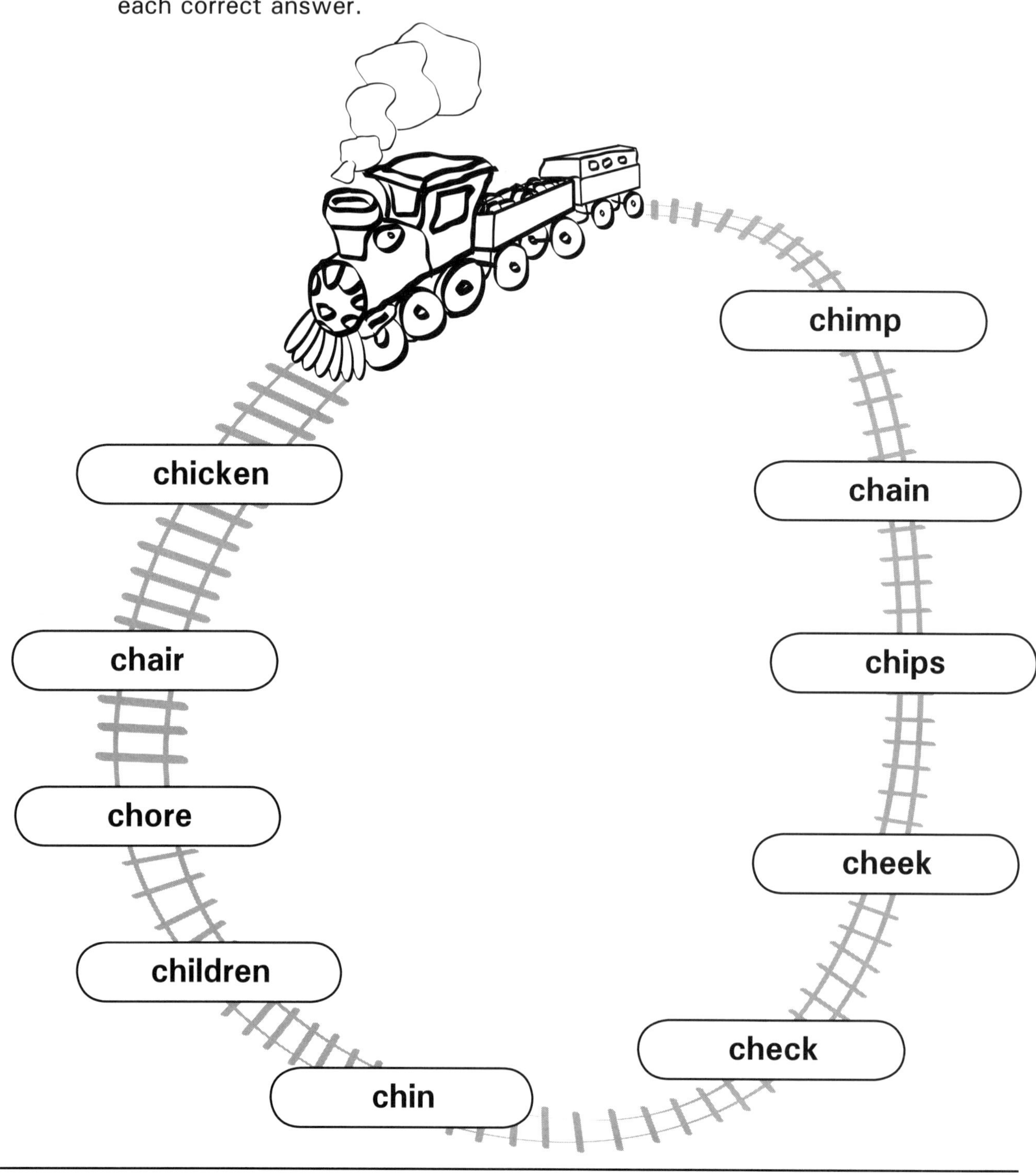

CH Medial Single Words

Name: Date:

Directions: Say each word slowly. Make sure to elongate the medial ch sound. Mark the speech/homework block as appropriate for correct pronunciation.

teacher

Speech ___ Homework ___

beach ball

Speech ___ Homework ___

marching

Speech ___ Homework ___

pitcher

Speech ___ Homework ___

fire chief

Speech ___ Homework ___

touchdown

Speech ___ Homework ___

wheelchair

Speech ___ Homework ___

inchworm

Speech ___ Homework ___

More CH Medial Practice Words:

urchin
artichoke
Archie
woodchuck
searching
Gretchen
merchant
preaches

CH Medial Phrases

Name: Date:

Directions: Say each phrase slowly. Make sure to elongate the medial ch sound. Mark the speech/homework block as appropriate for correct pronunciation.

Play with a beach ball.

Speech ___ Homework ___

In the kitchen.

Speech ___ Homework ___

First grade teacher.

Speech ___ Homework ___

Pass the ketchup.

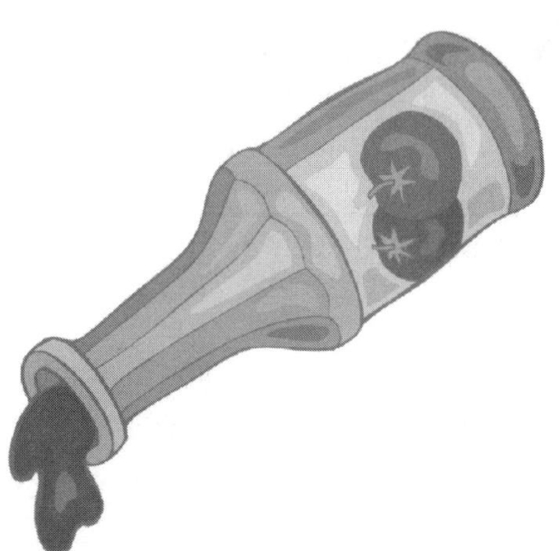

Speech ___ Homework ___

Hatching dinosaur.	The small inchworm.

Speech ___ Homework ___	Speech ___ Homework ___
A fortune cookie.	The brave firechief.

Speech ___ Homework ___	Speech ___ Homework ___

More CH Medial Practice Phrases:

A sea urchin.
The artichoke.
Archie the cat.
A winning touchdown.

Relief pitcher.
Gretchen is home.
The merchant.
Catching a ball.

CH Medial Sentences

Name: Date:

Directions: Say each sentence slowly. Cycle through each set, changing the ending for a different ch target word. Mark the speech/homework block as appropriate for correct pronunciation.

Archie saw the... Speech _ _ _ Homework _ _ _

pitcher

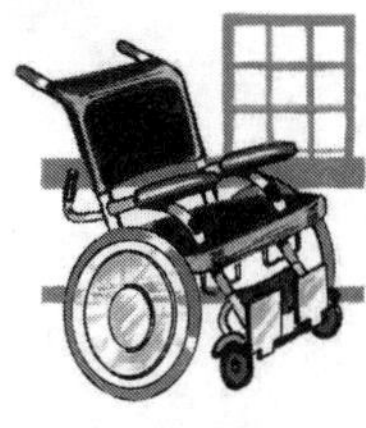

wheelchair

urchin

Richie liked the... Speech _ _ _ Homework _ _ _

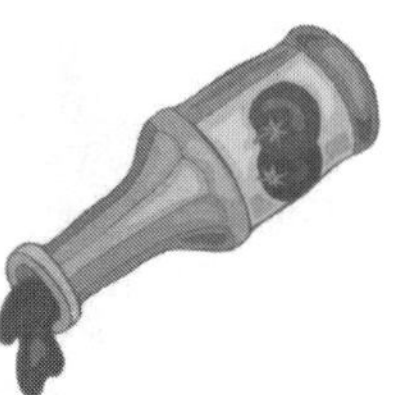

ketchup

marching band

teacher

Speech _ _ _ Homework _ _ _

Rachael made a...

fortune

touchdown

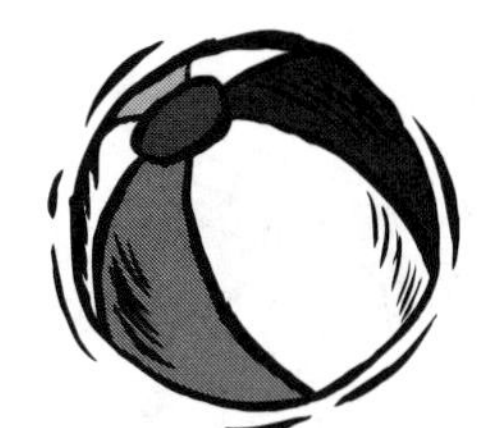

beach ball picture

CH Medial Activity: Matching

Name: Date:

Directions: Circle the picture that best belongs with the first one. Say each word aloud for practice.

Activity: Color In

Name: Date:

Directions: The instructor should make up a word list. Instruct the student to pronounce each word. For each correct answer, the student colors in a section of the inch worm. For each incorrect answer, the instructor colors in a section of the inch worm.

CH Medial Activity: Pitcher/Catcher

Name: Date:

Directions: Place a coin on the pitcher's mound to represent a baseball. The instructor slides the coin to the catcher and says "I'm pitching the ball." The student says "I'm catching the ball," and slides the coin back to the pitcher's mound. Repeat several times and then speed up keeping correct pronunciation.

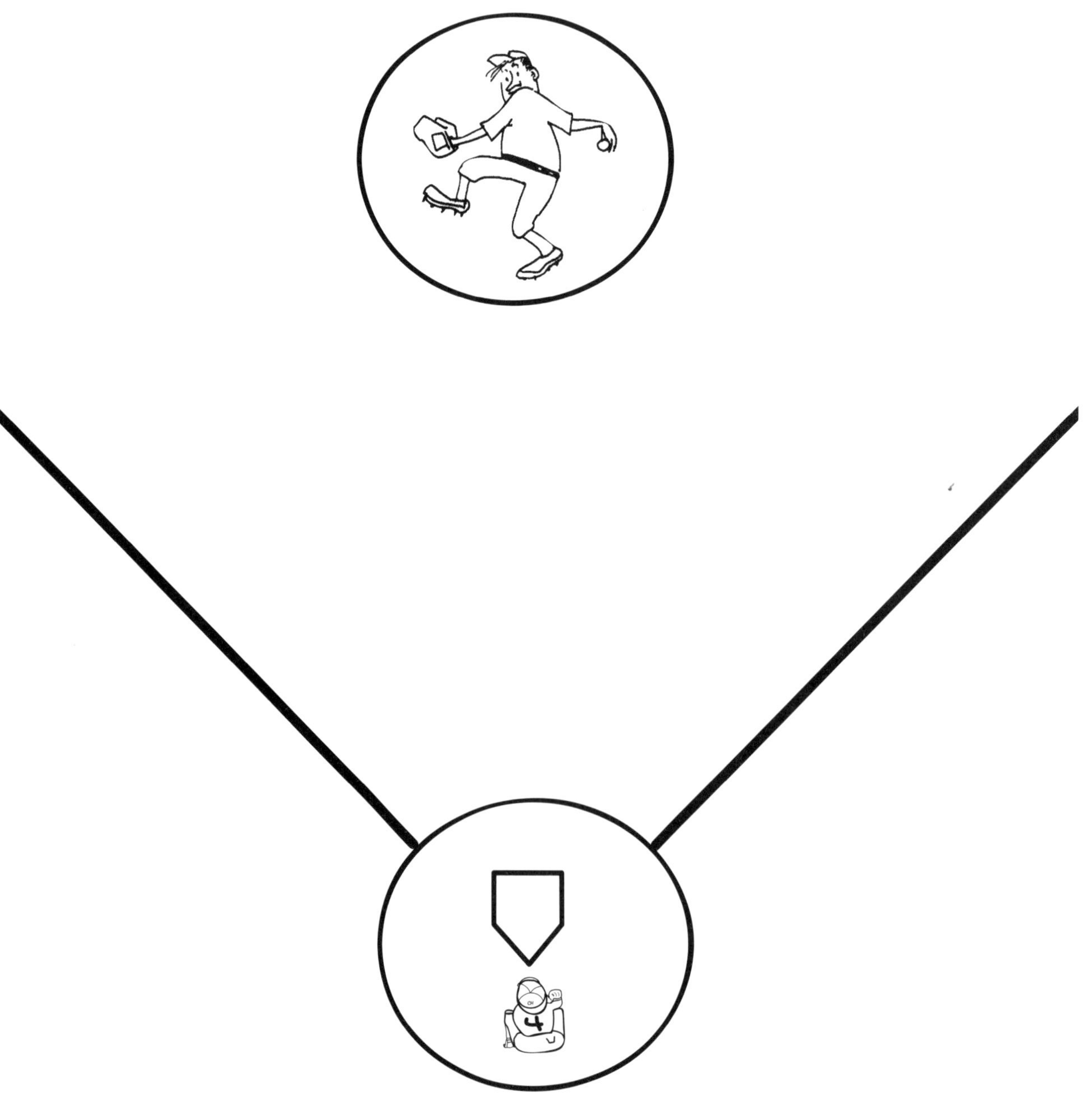

CH Final Single Words

Name: Date:

Directions: Say each word slowly. Make sure to elongate the final ch sound. Mark the speech/homework block as appropriate for correct pronunciation.

porch

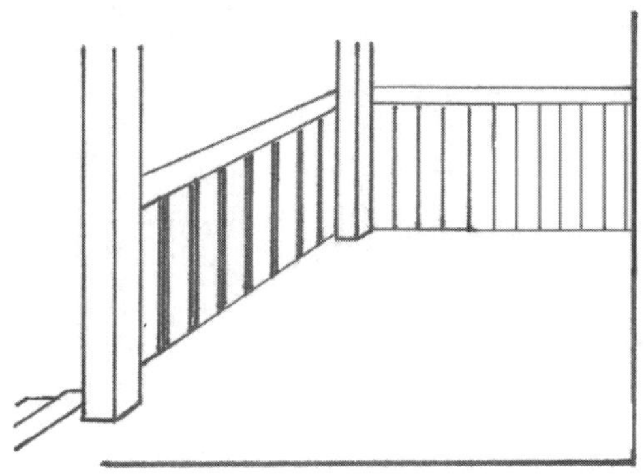

Speech ___ Homework ___

couch

Speech ___ Homework ___

peach

Speech ___ Homework ___

watch

Speech ___ Homework ___

catch

Speech ___ Homework ___

lunch

Speech ___ Homework ___

pinch

Speech ___ Homework ___

bench

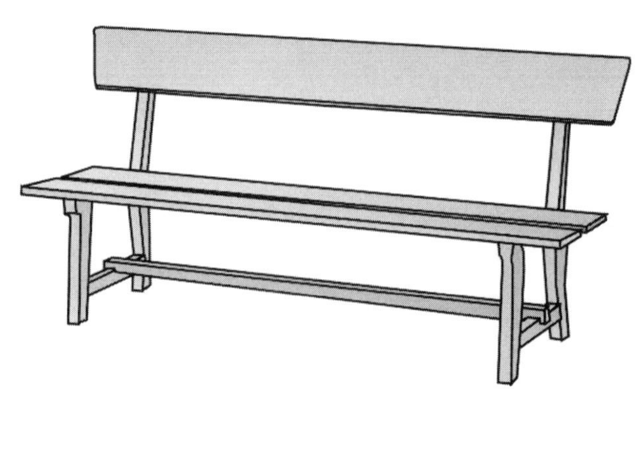

Speech ___ Homework ___

More CH Final Practice Words:

witch
perch
roach
latch

sandwich
patch
such
speech

CH Final Phrases

Name: Date:

Directions: Say each phrase slowly. Make sure to elongate the final ch sound. Mark the speech/homework block as appropriate for correct pronunciation.

Go to the beach.

Speech ___ Homework ___

Wear a watch.

Speech ___ Homework ___

A rich man.

Speech ___ Homework ___

A kangaroo's pouch.

Speech ___ Homework ___

A park bench.

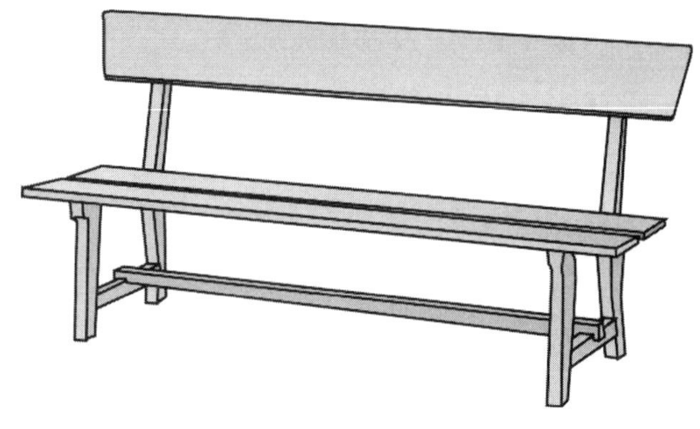

Speech ___ Homework ___

The men march.

Speech ___ Homework ___

An inch ruler.

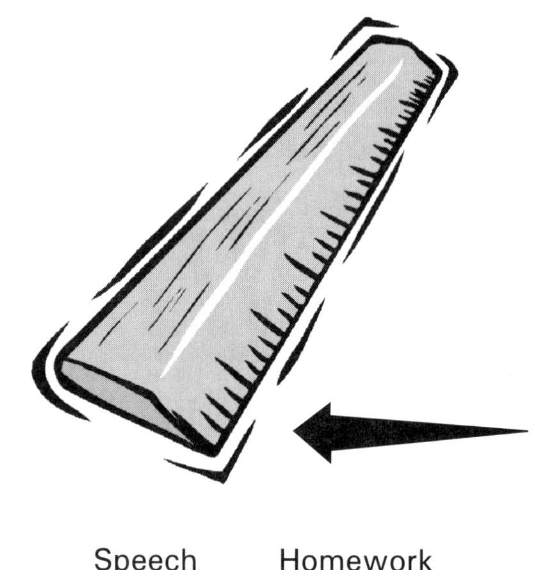

Speech ___ Homework ___

Ouch, a pinch.

Speech ___ Homework ___

More CH Final Practice Phrases:

Wicked witch.
Tall perch.
Ugly roach.
Open the latch.
Cheese sandwich.
Shoulder patch.
Such is life.
Good speech.

CH Final Sentences

Name: Date:

Directions: Say each sentence slowly. Cycle through each set, changing the ending for a different ch target word. Mark the speech/homework block as appropriate for correct pronunciation.

Mitch ate lunch on the... Speech _ _ _ Homework _ _ _

beach

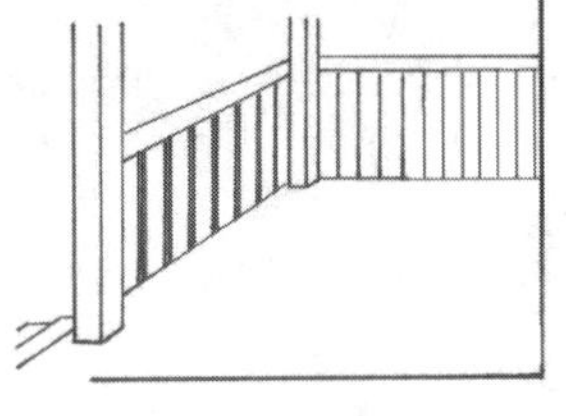
porch

couch

Blanche likes... Speech _ _ _ Homework _ _ _

to march

a sandwich

the pumpkin patch

Speech _ _ _ Homework _ _ _

Rich used the...

mitt to play catch

watch

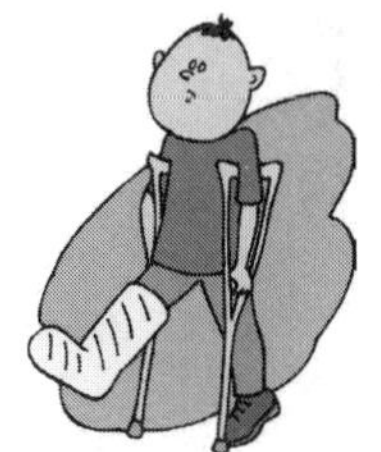
crutch

CH Final Activity: Beach Day

Name: Date:

Directions: Mitch and Sam went to the beach to have lunch. Circle the items in the picture that end in a "ch" sound.

CH Final Activity: Missing Letters

Name: Date:

Directions: Fill in the missing letters (hint:"ch"). Read each word aloud as the letters are filled in. Then, go back and read the story aloud for additional practice. If the students can't read, the instructor should read the story for phonemic awareness.

One day, Mit__ and Sam went to the bea__ to eat lun__.

In their lun__, they packed a sandwi__, a pea__, milk and cookies. When they got to the bea__, they sat down on a ben__ and began to eat lun__.

After lun__, Sam asked Mit__, "What is the time?" Mit__ looked at his wat__ and told Sam it was 12:30pm.

Sam knew she would be late for soccer practice. Her coa__ and the other players would be waiting for her. Sam quickly cleaned up her lun__ and said good bye to Mit__. Later, Sam felt very full, because she had eaten too mu__ lun__!

CH Hopscotch

Name: Date:

Directions: Place index finger on box #1, say the word ("catch"). "Jump" to box #2, by placing index finger on that box and say the word ("chimney"). Continue jumping and pronouncing the words till box #10. Then turnaround and repeat the game.

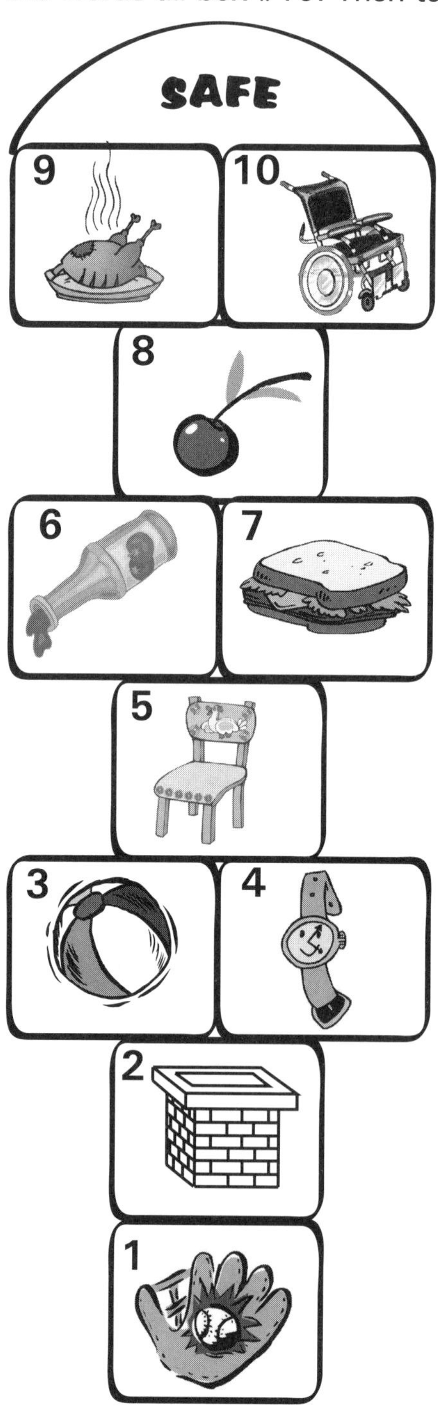

CHAPTER 6:

The Entire World™ of...

Initial, Medial & Final

J Teaching Tool

The /ʤ/ or j phoneme, commonly spelled with a j, g or dg as in ***j***am or bri***dg***e, is a voiced stop affricate. The j is the voiced cognate of ch therefore, it is produced exactly as ch is created, except that the sound is voiced (vocal cords vibrate).

The j is created using the /d/ + zh instead of the /t/ + sh (as for ch). Importantly, only the beginning or "stop" portion of /d/ is to be used. If the sound is carried through to the full "plosive" phase, then the phonemic approximation is lost.

The sound is created by the tongue tip touching the palato-alveolar region to stop the flow of air. The sound is initiated by the tongue tip quickly lowering and releasing the airflow. The sides of the tongue should be pressed against the upper back teeth forcing the airflow over the tongue. The lips are slightly protruded and the corners of the mouth are tensed.

The j phoneme is difficult to produce. The mechanics of forming j, both point of contact and width of the tongue, may vary depending on the context of the word in which it appears. Also, when the sound is voiced (i.e. voice box turned on) depends on placement and context. The final j begins with voice and ends without vibration as the vocal cords stop before the sound is completed. In the initial position, the opposite is true, the sound momentarily begins without voice and ends with voice.

Once ch is successfully attained, informing the student to "turn on" his voice box is sometimes all it takes for correct production. If that doesn't work, try the combination d final + y initial (e.g. rea**d** **y**our) exercises found on page 103 to stimulate production. Instruct the student to read this at a normal pace and then speed up the words to elicit the distinctive j sound.

Once the student has placement, reinforce the j sound by using "D Final + J Initial" and "J Final + J Initial" combination worksheets found on pages 105-111. Use the worksheets which place the phoneme in isolation or in isolated phrases for additional practice.

Therapeutic Tips for J

Involve as many senses as possible when teaching a student to correct an articulation/phonological disorder. Different modalities all contribute to a successful learning situation. Visual and tactile stimuli reinforce and complement auditory cueing techniques.

The following are a few ideas to try with your students. We encourage you to develop some of your own. Most importantly, use all of the tips simultaneously for maximum impact.

Auditory Tips

Refer to the j as the "jump sound" as in a jump rope. Use the auditory cue of a "thump" as in jumping rope. This will promote sound association when producing a j in jump.

Ear training exercises should be incorporated into therapy, since j is a complex sound. The more auditory experience that the student has with the sound the better. Try reading stories or target word lists to the student to enhance phonemic awareness, especially the voicing aspect.

Try the drill: *Bu, Du, Ju.* This sequence causes the tongue to move sound production from the front to the back of the mouth while emphasizing the plosive release of airflow and vocal cord vibration. Repeat and speed up until mastered.

Visual Tips

Make a copy of the large "J" on page 101. Place this cue in front of the student at every session as a visual reference.

Another visual cue is to extend your hand out and move your arm and hand quickly as making the shape of the letter "J" as you make the j sound. Emphasize the plosive phase of the pronunciation with the visual cue of your hand "jumping" up. Release the airflow at the bottom of the "J" as in Figure 6-1.

Instruct your students to remember the "jump sound" when producing the j. Perform this cue for students when they are first learning how to produce the j and as reinforcement later when your students are having difficulty with the j sound.

Figure 6-1 *"J" visual cue*

Use a mirror so the student can see proper mouth and lip positioning.

As with the ch, emphasize the explosive nature of j, by putting your hand in a fist. At the plosive stage (breath release) extend your hand showing all five fingers as you make the j sound. This visual cue is demonstrated in Figures 6-2 and 6-3.

Tactile Tips

Get a jump rope and have the student jump rope. Instruct the student to say "jump" each time he jumps. Actually touching the rope and jumping provides tactile or kinesthetic cueing, which stimulates learning.

Model the j sound for the student and instruct him to mimic you. As the tongue pushes off against the roof of the mouth at the initiation of the j sound, the jaw opens and the tongue drops. Instruct the student to place his hands on his jaw while making the sound for tactile reinforcement.

Another tactile cue is to instruct the student to color in the letters on the J worksheets found on page 102. The process of coloring focuses the student on the j sound while providing tactile reinforcement. It also provides a visual representation of the j phoneme. For additional tactile sensations, you can use glue and sprinkle glitter on the letters, trace the letters on a separate sheet of paper, or cut them out with scissors.

For the initial, medial and final single word and phrase worksheets, instruct the student to color in the pictures. Also, cut the pictures out and arrange them into a booklet or use as flash cards for games and memory exercises. (See page 36.)

Remediation Tricks

1. Instructing the student to give a quick, tight zh is sometimes effective in producing j.

2. Try directing the student to say /d/ + /z/ quickly until it sounds like j. For example, say dessert, first slowly separating the "d" from the "sert," then speeding up so the /d/ and

/z/ sounds are combined; dessert, dessert, dessert, dessert, etc.

3. If vocal cords do not vibrate or ch is substituted for j, use tactile stimulation. Place the student's hand on your voice box and model the sound. Instruct the student to place his hand on his voice box while making the sound.

4. As with the other sibilant sounds if the student's tongue is protruding to make a voiceless th or if airflow is leaking laterally, then the student may have a frontal or lateral lisp disorder. Use a mirror to demonstrate proper mouth and tongue positioning. Review the tips and techniques for frontal and lateral lisps in ***The Entire World of S & Z™ Instructional Workbook.***

5. If the student's tongue is too narrow and allowing lateral airflow, try widening it by encouraging the student to make a voiced th.

Figure 6-1 *Visual cue for j at stop*

Figure 6-2 *Visual cue for j at plosive release*

J Activity: Jump Rope

Name: Date:

Directions: Color in the girl jumping rope. Discuss what the girl is doing while your color.

Big J

Name: Date:

Directions: Color in the big "J." This activity provides tactile and visual stimulation when producing the j sound.

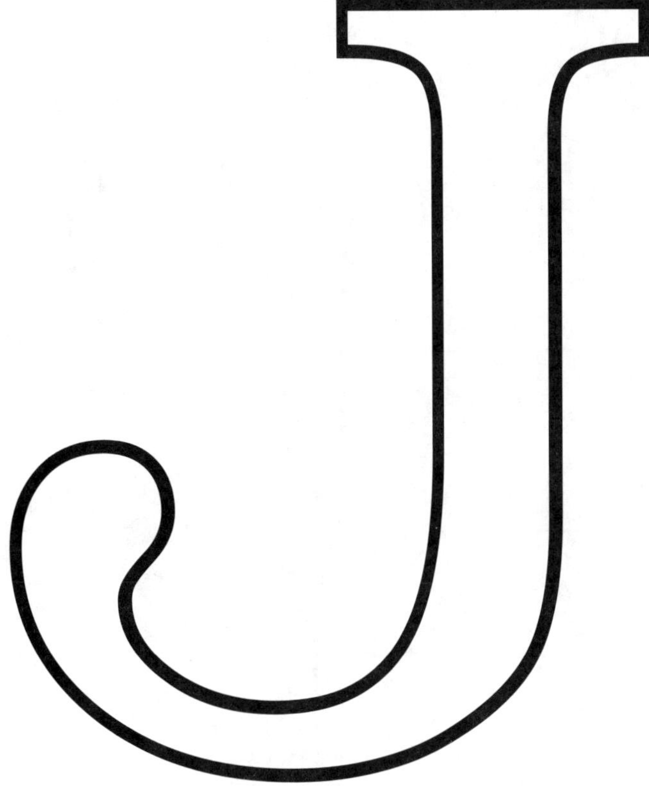

J Activity: JJJJ

Name: Date:

Directions: The instructor should make up a word list. Instruct the student to pronounce the j words. If correct, the student gets to color in an "J." If incorrect, the instructor colors in a "J." Continue until all the letters are colored.

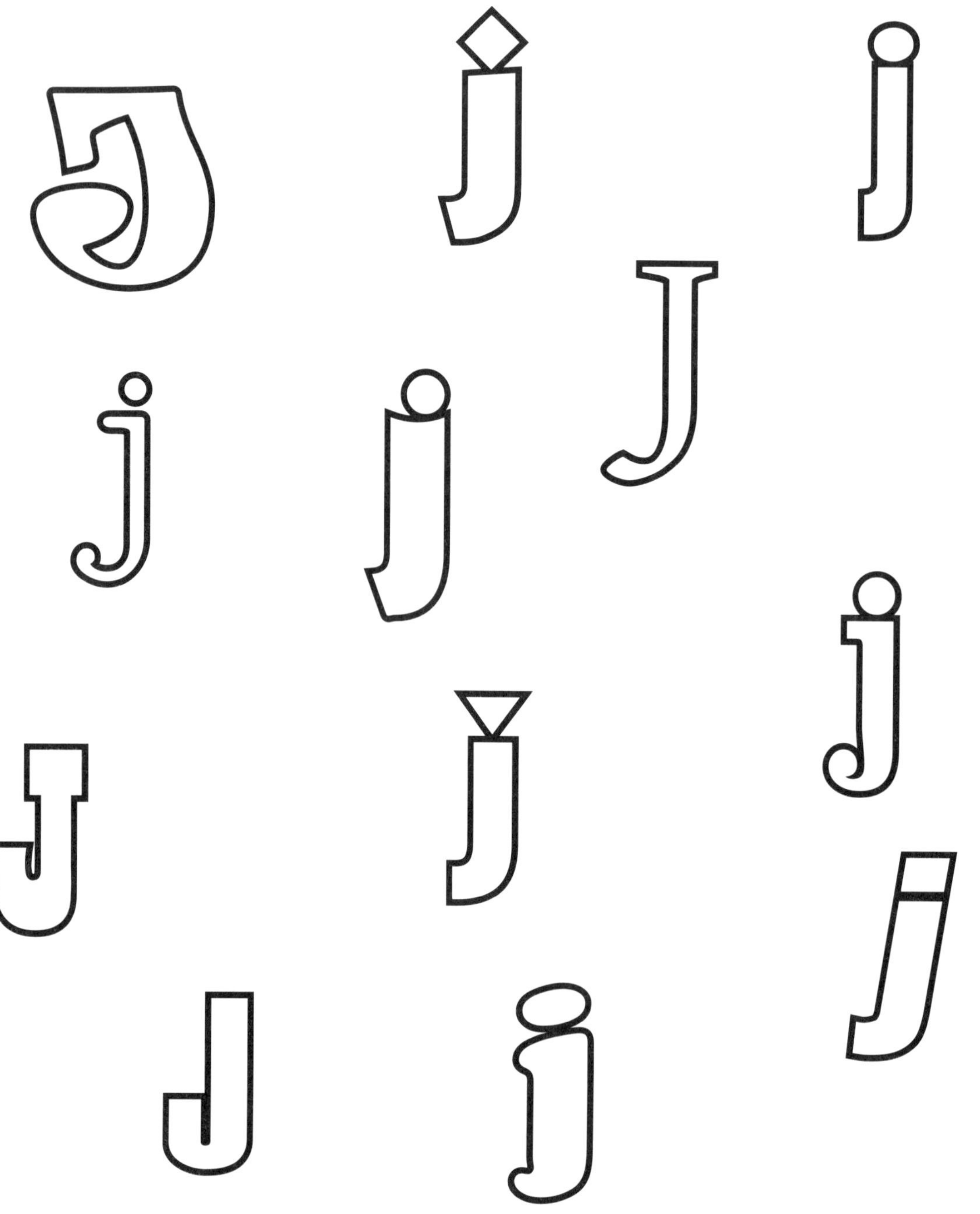

D Final + Y Initial

Elicitation Phrases

Name: Date:

Directions: Use this exercise if the student cannot produce j. Say each phrase slowly. The d final + y initial combination creates a j medial word. Mark the speech/homework block as appropriate for correct pronunciation.

	Speech	Homework
1). Rea**d** **y**our book.	______	______
2). Plea**d** **y**our case.	______	______
3). Fee**d** **y**ourselves.	______	______
4). Di**d** **y**ou go?	______	______
5). Ma**de** **y**ou a star.	______	______
6). Sen**d** **y**ou a letter.	______	______
7). Mende**d** **y**our pants.	______	______
8). Blende**d** **y**our milk.	______	______
9). Ma**de** **y**ou go.	______	______
10). Di**d** **y**ou study?	______	______
11). Coul**d** **y**ou call?	______	______
12). The bearde**d** **y**ak.	______	______

D Final + Y Initial
Elicitation Sentences

Name: Date:

Directions: Use this exercise if the student cannot produce j. The d final + y initial combination creates a j medial word. Say each sentence slowly. Mark the speech/homework block as appropriate for correct pronunciation.

	Speech	Homework
1). You need to rea**d** **y**our book.	_____	_____
2). You are free to plea**d** **y**our case.	_____	_____
3). Please fee**d** **y**ourselves.	_____	_____
4). Di**d** **y**ou go to the party?	_____	_____
5). The TV ma**de** **y**ou a star.	_____	_____
6). Julie is going to sen**d** **y**ou a letter.	_____	_____
7). Belinda mende**d** **y**our pants.	_____	_____
8). Patsy blende**d** **y**our milk.	_____	_____
9). Brenda ma**de** **y**ou go to the party.	_____	_____
10). Di**d** **y**ou study for the test?	_____	_____
11). Coul**d** **y**ou call for me?	_____	_____
12). The bearde**d** **y**ak runs free.	_____	_____

D Final + J Initial

Elicitation Phrases

Name: Date:

Directions: Use this exercise to obtain production of j medial. Say each phrase slowly; then repeat and speed up production. Mark the speech/homework block as appropriate for correct pronunciation.

	Speech	Homework
1). Plaid jacket.	______	______
2). Suede jeans.	______	______
3). Did Jean go?	______	______
4). Mixed jam.	______	______
5). Could Jeff.	______	______
6). Would jazz be okay?	______	______
7). The spoiled juice.	______	______
8). World geography.	______	______
9). The spotted giraffe.	______	______
10). The grand general.	______	______
11). Soiled gym clothes.	______	______
12). The speed jet.	______	______

D Final + J Initial Phrases
With J Initial in Isolation

Name: Date:

Directions: Use d to get j. Say each sentence slowly, pause and say the j initial word in isolation. Emphasis should be on a clean crisp j. Mark the speech homework block as appropriate for correct pronunciation.

	Speech	Homework
1). Plai**d** **j**acket. ⇨ **j**acket	______	______
2). Sue**de** **j**eans. ⇨ **j**eans	______	______
3). Di**d** **J**ean go. ⇨ **J**ean	______	______
4). Mixe**d** **j**am. ⇨ **j**am	______	______
5). Coul**d** **J**eff. ⇨ **J**eff	______	______
6). Woul**d** **j**azz be okay. ⇨ **j**azz	______	______
7). The spoile**d** **j**uice. ⇨ **j**uice	______	______
8). Worl**d** **g**eography. ⇨ **g**eography	______	______
9). The spotte**d** **g**iraffe. ⇨ **g**iraffe	______	______
10). The gran**d** **g**eneral. ⇨ **g**eneral	______	______
11). Soile**d** **g**ym clothes. ⇨ **g**ym	______	______
12). The spee**d** **j**et. ⇨ **j**et	______	______

D Final + J Initial Sentences

With J Initial in Isolation

Name: Date:

Directions: This exercise uses d final to assist in producing j initial. Say each sentence slowly; pause, then say the sentence with the j initial word in isolation. Mark the speech/homework block as appropriate.

	Speech	Homework
1). The plaid jacket was mine.	______	______
⇨ The jacket was mine.	______	______
2). Tina bought the suede jeans.	______	______
⇨ Tina bought the jeans.	______	______
3). Did Jean go to the game?	______	______
⇨ Jean went to the game.	______	______
4). Darby put mixed jam on her toast.	______	______
⇨ Darby put jam on the toast.	______	______
5). Could Jeff be the captain?	______	______
⇨ Jeff is the captain.	______	______
6). Would jazz be okay to listen to?	______	______
⇨ Jazz is fun to listen to.	______	______
7). The spoiled juice was poured out.	______	______
⇨ The juice was poured out.	______	______
8). World geography is my favorite class.	______	______
⇨ Geography is my favorite class.	______	______

Using J Final to Produce J Initial

Elicitation Phrases

Name: Date:

Directions: Say each phrase slowly; then repeat and speed up production. Emphasis is on obtaining correct production of j initial from a correct j final. Mark the speech/homework block as appropriate for correct pronunciation.

	Speech	Homework
1). The villa**ge** **g**ypsy.	______	______
2). Ur**ge** **J**odi to go.	______	______
3). Voya**ge** **j**et.	______	______
4). Cotta**ge** **g**ym.	______	______
5). A funny marria**ge** **j**oke.	______	______
6). Fancy loun**ge** **j**acket.	______	______
7). Arran**ge** **J**odi's schedule.	______	______
8). Oran**ge** **j**uice.	______	______
9). An oran**ge** **j**eep.	______	______
10). The stora**ge** **j**ar.	______	______
11). Exchan**ge** **g**eometry answers.	______	______
12). Please pa**ge** **J**ustine.	______	______

Using J Final to Produce J Initial

Elicitation Sentences

Name: Date:

Directions: Say each sentence slowly; then repeat and speed up production. Emphasis is on obtaining correct production of j initial from a correct j final. Mark the speech/homework block as appropriate for correct pronunciation.

	Speech	Homework
1). The villa**ge** **g**ypsy is nice.	______	______
2). Ur**ge** **J**odi to go to the party.	______	______
3). The voya**ge** **j**et took us to Boston.	______	______
4). Sue lifted weights in the cotta**ge** **g**ym.	______	______
5). We told a funny marria**ge** **j**oke.	______	______
6). Tom wore his fancy loun**ge** **j**acket.	______	______
7). We need to arran**ge** **J**odi's schedule.	______	______
8). I drink oran**ge** **j**uice every morning.	______	______
9). We rode in the oran**ge** **j**eep.	______	______
10). We put the bugs in a stora**ge** **j**ar.	______	______
11). Please exchan**ge** **g**eometry answers for grading.	______	______
12). Ned needs to pa**ge** **J**ustine on the loudspeaker.	______	______

Using J Final to Produce J Initial

With J in Isolation

Name: Date:

Directions: Say each phrase slowly, pause, then pronounce the j initial word in isolation. Mark the speech/homework block as appropriate for correct pronunciation.

	Speech	Homework
1). The village gypsy. ⇨ gypsy	_______	_______
2). Urge Jodi to go. ⇨ Jodi	_______	_______
3). Voyage jet. ⇨ jet	_______	_______
4). Cottage gym. ⇨ gym	_______	_______
5). A funny marriage joke. ⇨ joke	_______	_______
6). Fancy lounge jacket. ⇨ jacket	_______	_______
7). Arrange Jodi's schedule. ⇨ Jodi's schedule	_______	_______
8). Orange juice. ⇨ juice	_______	_______
9). An orange jeep. ⇨ jeep	_______	_______
10). Storage jar. ⇨ jar	_______	_______
11). Exchange geometry answers. ⇨ geometry answers	_______	_______

Using J Final to Produce J Initial
With J Sentence in Isolation

Name: Date:

Directions: Say each sentence slowly, pause, then say the sentence with the j initial word in isolation. Mark the speech/homework block as appropriate for correct pronunciation.

	Speech	Homework
1). The villa**ge** **g**ypsy is nice. ⇨ The **g**ypsy was nice.	___	___
2). Ur**ge** **J**odi to go to the party. ⇨ **J**odi went to the party.	___	___
3). The voya**ge** **j**et took us to San Francisco. ⇨ The **j**et took us to San Francisco.	___	___
4). Sue lifted weights in the cotta**ge** **g**ym. ⇨ Sue lifted weights at the **g**ym.	___	___
5). We told a funny marria**ge** **j**oke. ⇨ The **j**oke was funny.	___	___
6). Tom wore his fancy loun**ge** **j**acket. ⇨ The **j**acket was fancy.	___	___
7). We need to arran**ge** **J**odi's schedule for today. ⇨ **J**odi's schedule is finished.	___	___
8). I drink oran**ge** **j**uice every morning. ⇨ Every morning I drink **j**uice.	___	___

J and CH Contrasts

Name: Date:

Directions: This exercise develops phonemic awareness and sound discrimination by comparing j and ch words using similar phonetic contexts. Instruct the student to say the word in the left column and then the right. Describe why the words are the same or different. Make a copy, cut out the boxes and mix up the words for more practice.

		Same	Different
arrange	approach	______	______
match	Madge	______	______
cheap	jeep	______	______
chump	jump	______	______
Joyce	choice	______	______
Jarred	chaired	______	______
choke	joke	______	______
catch	cage	______	______
lunge	lunch	______	______
badge	batch	______	______
etch	edge	______	______
ridge	rich	______	______

J Initial Single Words

Name: Date:

Directions: Say each word slowly. Make sure to elongate the initial j sound. Mark the speech/homework block as appropriate for correct pronunciation.

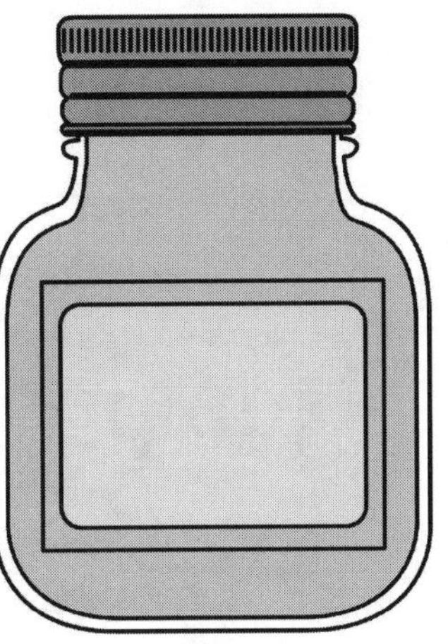

Speech ___ Homework ___

Speech ___ Homework ___

jacket

Speech ___ Homework ___

juice

Speech ___ Homework ___

jewelry

Speech ___ Homework ___

giraffe

Speech ___ Homework ___

jack in the box

Speech ___ Homework ___

jump

Speech ___ Homework ___

More J Initial Practice Words:

gem
jam
gym
jazz

jellybean
joke
junk
Jimmy

J Initial Phrases

Name: Date:

Directions: Say each phrase slowly. Make sure to elongate the initial j sound. Mark the speech/homework block as appropriate for correct pronunciation.

Drink juice.

Speech ___ Homework ___

Peanut butter and jelly.

Speech ___ Homework ___

A jet plane.

Speech ___ Homework ___

A jar of jellybeans.

Speech ___ Homework ___

Pretty jewelry.

Speech ___ Homework ___

Jump higher.

Speech ___ Homework ___

The cookie jar.

Speech ___ Homework ___

The gentle giraffe.

Speech ___ Homework ___

More J Initial Practice Phrases:

Smart genius.
Jam and toast.
Gym shoes.
Jazz music.

Yellow jellybean.
Told a joke.
Junk drawer.
Jill and Jimmy.

J Initial Sentences

Name: Date:

Directions: Say each sentence slowly. Cycle through each set, changing the ending for a different j target word. Mark the speech/homework block as appropriate for correct pronunciation.

Joe bought the... Speech _ _ _ Homework _ _ _

juice jelly jewelry

Jackie likes the... Speech _ _ _ Homework _ _ _

jack in the box jacket gym

Speech _ _ _ Homework _ _ _

Jill saw the...

giraffe jet plane cookie jar

Activity: Color In Jack

Name: Date:

Directions: The instructor should make up a word list. Instruct the student to pronounce the words. For each correct answer, the student colors in a jack-in-the-box. For each incorrect answer, the instructor colors in a jack-in-the-box.

Activity: Circle the Word

Name: Date:

Directions: Circle the word in each box that most closely matches the picture. Say each word aloud.

Example: sandwich, blocks, jelly (circled)	soda, juice, butter	jellybeans, watermelon, frog	pants, jersey, shorts
jewelry, light bulb, pen	soap, cookie jar, salt	book, sit, jump	car, jet plane, boat
dog, elephant, giraffe	jacket, blanket, sunshine	table, gym, snake	jazz, fireman, cook

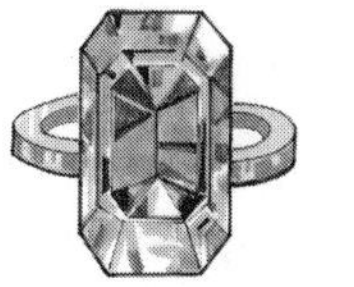

Activity: Circle the Word

J Initial Activity: Jar Matching

Name: Date:

Directions: Say the name of each item in the jar aloud. Draw a line connecting the matching pictures.

J Medial Single Words

Name: Date:

Directions: Say each word slowly. Make sure to elongate the medial j sound. Mark the speech/homework block as appropriate for correct pronunciation.

vegetables

Speech ___ Homework ___

magic

Speech ___ Homework ___

majorette

Speech ___ Homework ___

pager

Speech ___ Homework ___

engineer  Speech ___ Homework ___	soldier  Speech ___ Homework ___
education  Speech ___ Homework ___	fire engine  Speech ___ Homework ___

More J Medial Practice Words:

lodges	danger
ages	manger
surgeon	major
ranger	Benjamin

J Medial Phrases

Name: Date:

Directions: Say each phrase slowly. Make sure to elongate the medial j sound. Mark the speech/homework block as appropriate for correct pronunciation.

The majorette.

Speech ___ Homework ___

A pager.

Speech ___ Homework ___

magic trick.

Speech ___ Homework ___

A carrot is a vegetable.

Speech ___ Homework ___

The army jeep.

Speech ___ Homework ___

The train engineer.

Speech ___ Homework ___

A red fire engine.

Speech ___ Homework ___

A brave soldier.

Speech ___ Homework ___

More J Medial Practice Phrases:

Lodges in the mountains.
What are your ages?
Skilled surgeon.
Ranger Gidget.

Danger ahead!
Away in the manger.
A major deal.
Benjamin, the pidgeon.

J Medial Sentences

Name: Date:

Directions: Say each sentence slowly. Cycle through each set, changing the ending for a different j target word. Mark the speech/homework block as appropriate for correct pronunciation.

Margie is a...

Speech _ _ _ Homework _ _ _

majorette

soldier

passenger

The magician has... Speech _ _ _ Homework _ _ _

an urgent call

magic tricks

a pager

Speech _ _ _ Homework _ _ _

The engineer likes...

orangeade

vegetables

the army jeep

J Medial Activity: Toy Soldiers

Name: Date:

Directions: The instructor should make up a word list. The student should say each word aloud. For each word pronounced correctly, the student gets to color in a toy soldier. For each word incorrect, the instructor colors in a toy soldier.

J Medial Activity: Matching

Name: Date:

Directions: Say each sentence slowly. Circle the sentence that best describes each picture.

The magician is standing.

The magician is pulling a rabbit out of a hat.

The rabbit is eating vegetables.

The fire engine is going to a fire.

Fire engines are painted pink.

The fire engine is in the firehouse.

The engineer is in the caboose.

Two engineers are in the engine.

The engineer is running the engine.

The messenger is sitting.

Messengers move slow.

The messenger has an urgent message.

J Medial Activity: Matching

J Medial Activity: Story Time

Name: Date:

Directions: Read the word list below first; then read the story aloud. Say the word that represents each picture.

The  went to . He wanted to get an  in . It was 

for him to get an . He got a ride with his friend,  in her  He was the . For snacks he took some  and some .

 engineer

 Argentina

 education

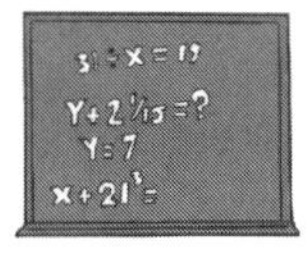 algebra

urgent

 Marge

 army jeep

 passenger

 vegetables

 orangeade

J Final Single Words

Name: Date:

Directions: Say each word slowly. Make sure to elongate the final j sound. Mark the speech/homework block as appropriate for correct pronunciation.

orange	bridge

Speech ___ Homework ___	Speech ___ Homework ___
badge	**cottage**

Speech ___ Homework ___	Speech ___ Homework ___

page	baggage
	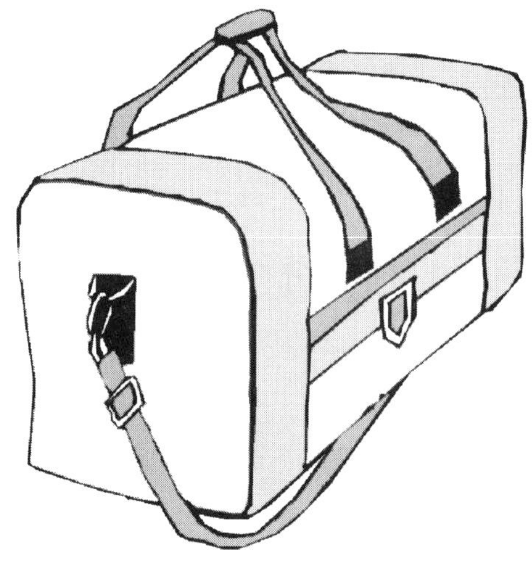
Speech ___ Homework ___	Speech ___ Homework ___
fudge	**cage**

Speech ___ Homework ___	Speech ___ Homework ___

More J Final Practice Words:

marriage	urge
judge	wedge
voyage	gauge
garbage	barge

J Final Phrases

Name: Date:

Directions: Say each phrase slowly. Make sure to elongate the final j sound. Mark the speech/homework block as appropriate for correct pronunciation.

A fudge sundae.

Speech ___ Homework ___

Take out the garbage.

Speech ___ Homework ___

On the stage.

Speech ___ Homework ___

The bridge.

Speech ___ Homework ___

In the cottage.

Speech ___ Homework ___

The bird cage.

Speech ___ Homework ___

Tear a page.

Speech ___ Homework ___

Message for you.

Speech ___ Homework ___

More J Final Practice Phrases:

Good marriage.
Wise judge.
Have a good voyage.
Hold a grudge.
The urge to go.
Drive a wedge.
The tire gauge.
A floating barge.

J Final Sentences

Name: Date:

Directions: Say each sentence slowly. Cycle through each set, changing the ending for a different j target word. Mark the speech/homework block as appropriate for correct pronunciation.

Marge has... Speech _ _ _ Homework _ _ _

an orange

a cottage

a new marriage

In the storage closet there is... Speech _ _ _ Homework _ _ _

a birdcage

badge

baggage

Speech _ _ _ Homework _ _ _

Paige went...

over the bridge

to get a message

to take out the garbage

J Final Sentences

J Final Activity: Matching

Name: Date:

Directions: Match the word in the column on the left with the word picture on the right that best matches. Say the words aloud for extra practice.

Activity: Badges

Name: Date:

Directions: The instructor should make up a word list. Instruct the student to pronounce the words. For each correct answer, the student colors in a badge. For each incorrect answer, the instructor colors in a badge.

Activity: The Stage

Name: Date:

Directions: You are the director of a stage play. Draw a scene from your play in the picture below. Get extra credit if you can use any j words in your play.

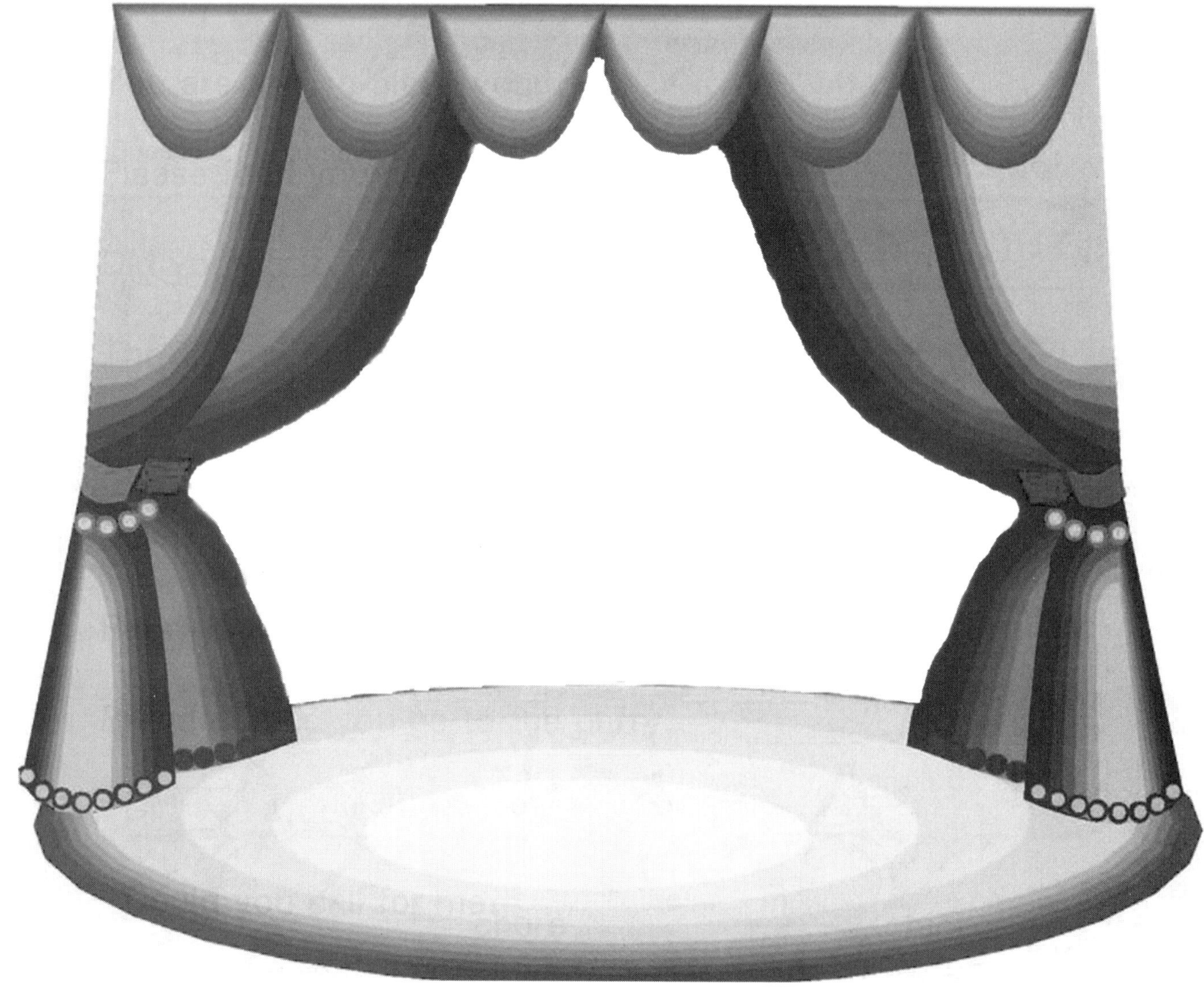

CHAPTER 7:

The Entire World™ of...

Initial, Medial & Final

SH

SH Teaching Tool

The /ʃ/ or sh phoneme is a continuant sibilant fricative consonant. There are two main components to its production--tongue placement and continuous airstream.

To produce the sh, the tongue tip points to, but does not touch, the hard palate or "roof of the mouth." In some cases the tongue tip may be pointing to the alveolar ridge (or just behind) which is the gum line behind the upper central incisors. The tongue should be curled back slightly and tensed to press against the sides of the upper back teeth.

The air stream is emitted centrally and is forced out over the tongue and through the teeth.

The lips are rounded and slightly protruded or pushed out. The teeth are partially separated. The corners of the mouth are also tightened. The vocal cords do not vibrate.

Production of this sound is similar to the production of the /s/ phoneme. Proper pronunciation of /s/ should be attained before attempting to correct the sh phoneme. This is to keep the lisping habits from interfering with the target sounds. Additionally, some of the approximate phonemic production zone assists that are used will not be effective.

If the student has already had success with ch, then one of the easiest methods for producing sh is to simply elongate the ch sound: "chshhhh". If that doesn't work, try the approximate phonemic production zone exercises found in this chapter. Start with "S Final + Y Initial Elicitation Phrases" on page 146 or "CH Final + SH Initial Elicitation Phrases" on page 149. Continue with the sentences and isolation exercises that follow.

Once sh final is attained, use the exercises starting on page 154 to help elicit sh medial and initial. Finally, use the single words, phrases, sentences, and activity sheets for sh initial, medial and final pronunciation starting on page 157.

Therapeutic Tips for SH

Involve as many senses as possible when teaching a student to correct an articulation/phonological disorder. Different modalities all contribute to a successful learning situation. Visual and tactile stimuli reinforce and complement auditory cueing techniques.

The following are a few ideas to try with your students. We encourage you to develop some of your own. Most importantly, use all of the tips simultaneously for maximum impact.

Auditory Tips

Refer to the sh as the "shhh sound" as in "being quiet" because the baby is sleeping." Associating the sound with the familiar gesture will aid the students in their production.

Practice the auditory contrast: *th, s sh.* Instruct the student to say this combination repeatedly and speed with success. This exercise moves the tongue in sequence from front to back. Combine it with a visual cue of the instructor's hand moving back to indicate the gradual withdrawal of the tongue moving back into the mouth.

Incorporate ear training into your therapy. Read the target words or stories with the target words to the student. Instruct her to raise her hand or identify the target sound when she hears the sound. Since the student is having difficulty producing the correct sound, the goal is to train her to listen for the correct sound.

Visual Tips

Make a copy of the large "SH" on page 144. Place this cue in front of the student at every session as a visual reference.

Use a mirror when teaching and correcting sh to show proper lip and mouth position.

As a complement to the auditory "shhhh sound," provide a visual model by holding your index finger up to your mouth/lips as if you are saying "be quiet" or shhh! This will be a vivid cue for the student, as most children are familiar with the motion and sounds for keeping quiet. See Figure 7-1.

Instruct your student(s) to remember

the "shhh sound" when producing the sh. Perform this cue for students when they are first learning how to

Figure 7-1 *Shhh sound*

produce sh and as a reinforcement when your students are having difficulty with the sh sound.

Another visual cue is to extend your hand and make a wave motion while modeling the sh sound. Do

Figure 7-2 *Wave cue*

this motion to reinforce airflow. See Figure 7-2.

Tactile Tips

Model the sh sound for the student. The mouth should be in a rounded position with the teeth showing. Point an index finger to the lips to demonstrate the "shhh sound." Instruct the student to use this cue to develop kinesthetic awareness of proper tongue positioning and air flow.

Another tactile cue is to instruct the student to color in the letters on the sh worksheets found on pages 144-145. The process of coloring focuses the student on the sh sound while providing tactile reinforcement. It also provides a visual representation of the sh phoneme.

For additional tactile sensations, you can use glue and sprinkle glitter on the letters, trace the letters on a separate sheet of paper, or cut them out with scissors.

For the initial, medial and final single word and phrase worksheets, starting on page 157, instruct the student to color in the pictures. Cut the pictures out and arrange into a booklet or use as flash cards for games and memory exercises. See page 36.

Remediation Tricks

1. Say /s/ then slide the tongue back until you hear a sh. Instruct the student to think of a baby sleeping as a reminder of the "shhhh" sound. Use a mirror to reinforce rounded lips.

2. Elongate the ch sound: chhshh.

3. Model /i/, as in "s<u>ee</u>" and "k<u>ey</u>." Raise the tongue up and backward, turn off the voice and keep the air flowing. As soon as the voice is off, the sh should emerge.

4. Instruct the student to say /n/, keeping alveolar contact and sliding the tongue back for the sh. Ensure that the sides of the tongue are in contact with the inner surface of the upper back teeth. This ensures that the airflow rolls along the center of the tongue between the hard palate and tongue.

5. Suggest to the student that she draw in her tongue like a turtle draws in its head to sleep. This withdrawal of the tongue may be enough to elicit sh from /s/.

6. Use a voiceless /r/. Instruct the student to make an /r/ (e.g. red). Hold the sound for a second and turnoff the voice box while maintaining airflow and tongue positioning. Clench teeth until they almost touch and slightly protrude the lips. It may be necessary to force extra air from the diaphragm, but an sh sound should emerge.

7. If the student's tongue is protruding enough that the voiceless th is substituted, then the student may have a frontal or lateral lisp disorder. Review the tips and techniques for frontal and lateral lisp disorders in ***The Entire World of S & Z™ Instructional Workbook.***

SH & S Contrasts

Name: Date:

Directions: This exercise develops phonemic awareness and sound discrimination by comparing sh and s words using similar phonetic contexts. Instruct the student to say the word in the left column and then the right. Describe why the words are the same or different. Make a copy, cut out the boxes and mix up the words for more practice.

		Same	Different
sun	shun	______	______
show	sew	______	______
see	she	______	______
short	sort	______	______
sue	shoe	______	______
shelf	self	______	______
sheep	seep	______	______
sour	shower	______	______
sip	ship	______	______
shed	said	______	______
sift	shift	______	______
shoot	suit	______	______

SH & CH Contrasts

Name: Date:

Directions: This exercise develops phonemic awareness and sound discrimination by comparing sh and ch words using similar phonetic contexts. Instruct the student to say the word in the left column and then the right. Describe why the words are the same or different. Make a copy, cut out the boxes and mix up the words for more practice.

		Same	Different
share	chair	______	______
shoe	chew	______	______
mush	much	______	______
sheet	cheat	______	______
wash	watch	______	______
watching	washing	______	______
chop	shop	______	______
catch	cash	______	______
rash	ratchet	______	______
shore	chore	______	______
leash	leach	______	______
chime	shine	______	______

Big SH

Name: Date:

Directions: Color in the big "SH." This activity provides tactile and visual stimulation when producing the sh sound.

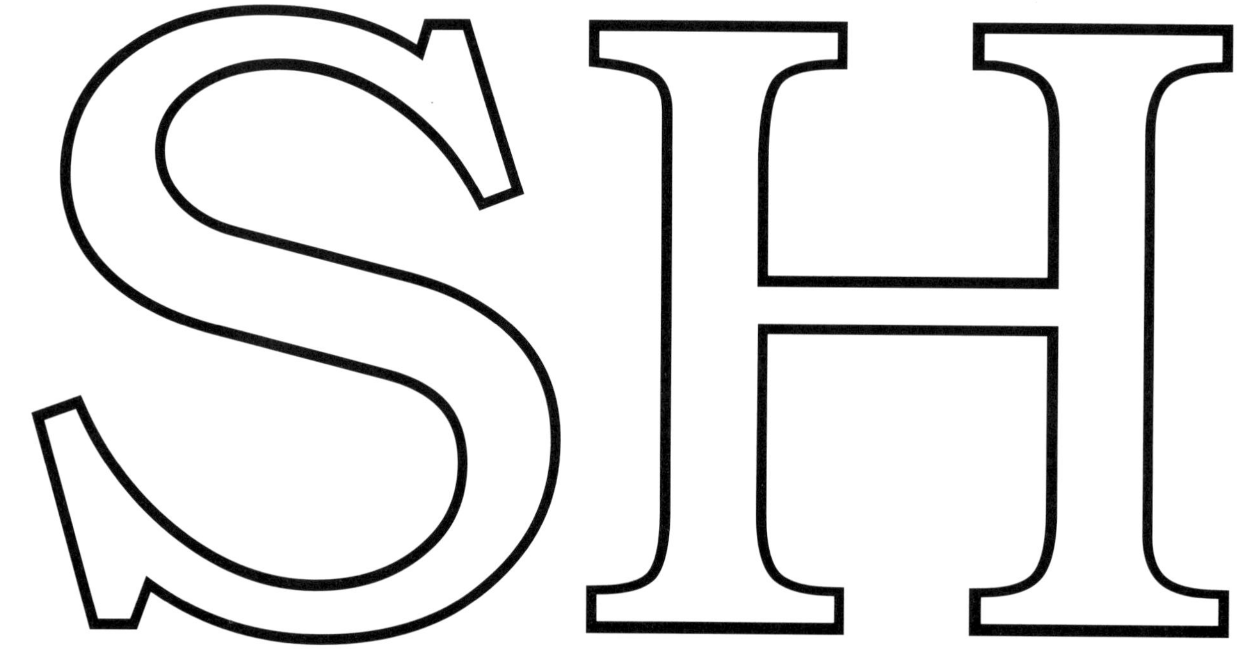

SH Activity: Shhhhh

Name: Date:

Directions: The instructor should make up a word list. Instruct the student to pronounce the sh words. If correct, the student gets to color in a "SH." If incorrect, the instructor colors in a "SH." Continue until all the letters are colored.

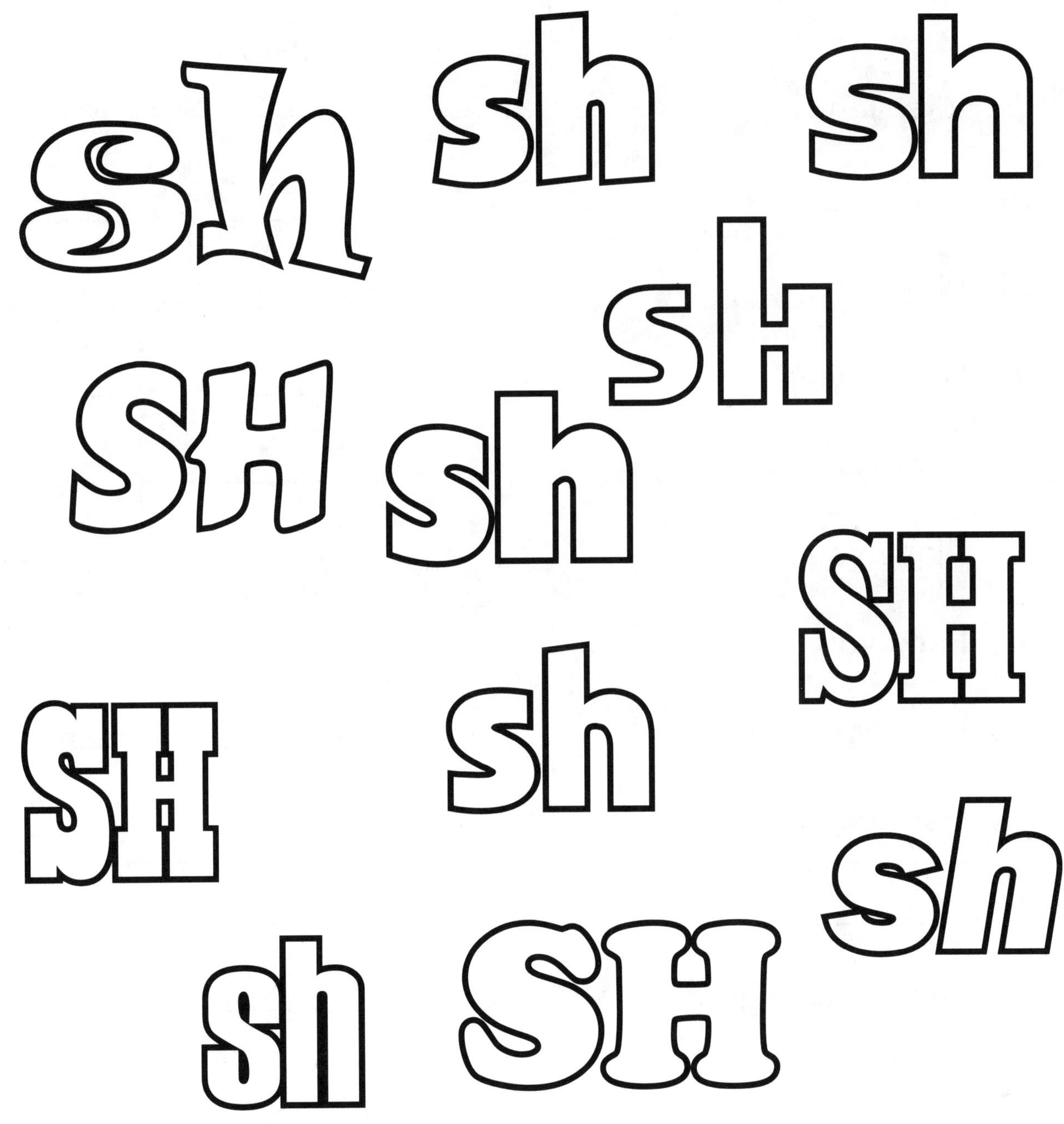

S Final + Y Initial

Elicitation Phrases to Produce SH Medial

Name: Date:

Directions: Use this exercise if neither sh or ch are producible. Say each phrase slowly. Elongate the final s for the transition to the y. Mark the speech/homework block as appropriate for correct pronunciation.

	Speech	Homework
1). Kiss you.	_______	_______
2). Miss you.	_______	_______
3). Bless you.	_______	_______
4). Unless you.	_______	_______
5). Address you.	_______	_______
6). Place you.	_______	_______
7). Face you.	_______	_______
8). Embrace you.	_______	_______
9). Replace you.	_______	_______
10). Advance you.	_______	_______
11). Romance you.	_______	_______
12). Dismiss you.	_______	_______

S Final + Y Initial

Elicitation Phrases With "shoe" in Isolation

Name: Date:

Directions: Say each phrase slowly. Elongate the final s for transition to the y; pause and then pronounce "shoe." Emphasis is on a clear sh. Mark the speech/homework block as appropriate for correct pronunciation.

	Speech	Homework
1). Kis**s** **y**ou. ⇨ shoe	______	______
2). Mis**s** **y**ou. ⇨ shoe	______	______
3). Bles**s** **y**ou. ⇨ shoe	______	______
4). Unles**s** **y**ou. ⇨ shoe	______	______
5). Addres**s** **y**ou. ⇨ shoe	______	______
6). Pla**ce** **y**ou. ⇨ shoe	______	______
7). Fa**ce** **y**ou. ⇨ shoe	______	______
8). Embra**ce** **y**ou. ⇨ shoe	______	______
9). Repla**ce** **y**ou. ⇨ shoe	______	______
10). Advan**ce** **y**ou. ⇨ shoe	______	______
11). Roman**ce** **y**ou. ⇨ shoe	______	______
12). Dismis**s** **y**ou. ⇨ shoe	______	______

S Final + Y Intial

Elicitation Sentences to Produce SH Medial

Name: Date:

Directions: Say each sentence slowly. Emphasis is on the transition from final s to initial y to form a medial sh. Mark the speech/homework block as appropriate for correct pronunciation.

	Speech	Homework
1). Mike will kis**s** **y**ou.		
2). I will mis**s** **y**ou.		
3). Ms. Taylor may dismis**s** **y**ou.		
4). Mis**s** **Y**ue is a lady.		
5). The teacher will addres**s** **y**ou.		
6). I will pla**ce** **y**ou next to Mary.		
7). I need to fa**ce** **y**ou.		
8). Mom will embra**ce** **y**ou.		
9). The boss may repla**ce** **y**ou.		
10). The principal may advan**ce** **y**ou.		
11). Your sweetie may roman**ce** **y**ou.		
12). Mom and Dad need to finan**ce** **y**our schooling.		

CH Final + SH Initial

Elicitation Phrases to Produce SH Medial

Name: Date:

Directions: Use this exercise if ch is correctly produced, but sh is not. Say each sentence slowly. Elongate the ch into the initial sh. Mark the speech/homework block as appropriate for correct pronunciation.

	Speech	Homework
1). Ea**ch** **sh**ark.	______	______
2). How mu**ch** **s**ugar.	______	______
3). Fren**ch** **sh**ampoo.	______	______
4). A bea**ch** **sh**ell.	______	______
5). Too mu**ch** **sh**rimp.	______	______
6). A lun**ch** **ch**ef.	______	______
7). The por**ch** **sh**ade.	______	______
8). Whi**ch** **sh**adow.	______	______
9). The Dut**ch** **sh**oe.	______	______
10). Whi**ch** **sh**oulder.	______	______
11). A ri**ch** **sh**eriff.	______	______
12). Pit**ch** **Sh**aron the ball.	______	______

CH Final + SH Initial

Elicitation Sentences to Produce SH Medial

Name: Date:

Directions: Use this exercise if ch is correctly produced, but sh is not. Say each sentence slowly. Elongate the ch into the initial sh. Mark the speech/homework block as appropriate for correct pronunciation.

	Speech	Homework
1). We looked at ea**ch** **sh**ark.	______	______
2). How mu**ch** **su**gar do we need?	______	______
3). Sally likes to use Fren**ch** **sh**ampoo.	______	______
4). The bea**ch** **sh**ell was pretty.	______	______
5). John ate too mu**ch** **sh**rimp.	______	______
6). We met the lun**ch** **ch**ef.	______	______
7). We sat under the por**ch** **sh**ade.	______	______
8). Whi**ch** **sh**adow do you see?	______	______
9). Pit**ch** **Sh**aron the softball.	______	______
10). Whi**ch** **sh**oulder did you hurt?	______	______
11). We met the ri**ch** **sh**eriff.	______	______
12). In Holland, Suzanne bought the Dut**ch** **sh**oe.	______	______

CH Final + SH Initial
With Initial SH in Isolation

Name: Date:

Directions: Use this exercise if ch is correctly produced, but sh is not. Say each sentence slowly. Elongate the ch into the initial sh. Mark the speech/homework block as appropriate for correct pronunciation.

	Speech	Homework
1). Ea**ch** **sh**ark. ⇨ **sh**ark	______	______
2). How mu**ch** **s**ugar. ⇨ **s**ugar	______	______
3). Fren**ch** **sh**ampoo. ⇨ **sh**ampoo	______	______
4). A bea**ch** **sh**ell. ⇨ **sh**ell	______	______
5). Too mu**ch** **sh**rimp. ⇨ **sh**rimp	______	______
6). A lun**ch** **ch**ef. ⇨ **ch**ef	______	______
7). The por**ch** **sh**ade. ⇨ **sh**ade	______	______
8). Whi**ch** **sh**adow. ⇨ **sh**adow	______	______
9). The Dut**ch** **sh**oe. ⇨ **sh**oe	______	______
10). Whi**ch** **sh**oulder. ⇨ **sh**oulder	______	______
11). A ri**ch** **sh**eriff. ⇨ **sh**eriff	______	______
12). Pit**ch** **Sh**aron the ball. ⇨ **Sh**aron	______	______

CH Final + SH Initial

Elicitation Sentence Pairs

Name: Date:

Directions: Say each sentence slowly. Cycle through each sentence pair. Elongate the ch into the initial sh in the "A" sentence. Emphasize the sh in isolation for the "B" sentence. Mark the speech/homework block as appropriate.

	Speech/	Homework
1A). We looked at ea**ch** **sh**ark.	____	____
1B). The **sh**arks looked at ea**ch** one of us.	____	____
2A). How mu**ch** **su**gar do we need?	____	____
2B). The **s**ugar we need seems to be too mu**ch**.	____	____
3A). Sally likes to use Fren**ch** **sh**ampoo.	____	____
3B). The **sh**ampoo that Sally uses is Fren**ch**.	____	____
4A). The bea**ch** **sh**ell was pretty.	____	____
4B). The **sh**ell from the bea**ch** is white.	____	____
5A). Ann ate too mu**ch** **sh**rimp.	____	____
5B). **Sh**rimp is good if you don't eat too mu**ch**.	____	____
6A). We met the lun**ch** **ch**ef at the restaurant.	____	____
6B). The **ch**ef who made our lun**ch** ate with us.	____	____

CH Final + SH Initial
Elicitation Sentence Pairs

Name: Date:

Directions: Say each sentence slowly. Cycle through each sentence pair. Elongate the ch into the initial sh in the "A" sentence. Emphasize the sh in isolation for the "B" sentence. Mark the speech/homework block as appropriate.

Speech/ Homework

7A). We sat under the por**ch** **sh**ade. ___ ___

7B). The **sh**ade under the por**ch** was cool. ___ ___

8A). Whi**ch** **sh**adow do you see? ___ ___

8B). The **sh**adow from the wit**ch** scared him. ___ ___

9A). Suzanne bought her bathing suit at the bea**ch** **sh**op. ___ ___

9B). The **sh**op has lots of good bea**ch** supplies. ___ ___

10A). Whi**ch** **sh**oulder did you hurt? ___ ___

10B). The right **sh**oulder hurts very mu**ch**. ___ ___

11A). Tea**ch** **Sh**erry how to make the cookies. ___ ___

11B). **Sh**erry wants to tea**ch** Mary how to make the cookies. ___ ___

12A). Pit**ch** **Sh**aron the softball. ___ ___

12B). **Sh**aron wants to pit**ch** the softball. ___ ___

Using SH Final

To Elicit SH Medial and SH Initial

Name: Date:

Directions: This exercise is designed to use a properly produced final sh to elicit medial sh and initial sh. Say each sentence slowly. Pause and pronounce the word in isolation. Mark the speech/homework block as appropriate for correct pronunciation.

	Speech	Homework
1). Spani**sh** **sh**ampoo. ⇨ **sh**ampoo	______	______
2). The bru**sh** **sh**op. ⇨ **sh**op	______	______
3). A starfi**sh** **sh**ell. ⇨ **sh**ell	______	______
4). A fre**sh** **sh**irt. ⇨ **sh**irt	______	______
5). Pu**sh** **Sh**eila. ⇨ **Sh**eila	______	______
6). Poli**sh** **sh**oes. ⇨ **sh**oes	______	______
7). Puni**sh** **Sh**elby. ⇨ **Sh**elby	______	______
8). Hu**sh** **Sh**aron. ⇨ **Sh**aron	______	______
9). A di**sh** **sh**elf. ⇨ **sh**elf	______	______
10). Tra**sh** **sh**ould go here. ⇨ **sh**ould	______	______
11). Squa**sh** **sh**oes. ⇨ **sh**oes	______	______
12). Ru**sh** **Sh**erry. ⇨ **Sh**erry	______	______

SH Final + SH Initial

Sentence Pairs

Name: Date:

Directions: Say each sentence slowly. Cycle through each sentence pair. Elongate the sh final into the initial sh in the "A" sentence. Emphasize the sh initial in isolation for the "B" sentence.

	Speech/	Homework
1A). We use Spani**sh** **sh**ampoo.	___	___
1B). **Sh**ampoo that is Spani**sh** works the best.	___	___
2A). Pu**sh** **Sh**eila in the wagon.	___	___
2B). **Sh**eila needs a pu**sh** in her wagon.	___	___
3A). We found a starfi**sh** **sh**ell.	___	___
3B). We found the **sh**ell from the starfi**sh**.	___	___
4A). Bill put on a fre**sh** **sh**irt.	___	___
4B). The **sh**irt that Bill is wearing is clean and fre**sh**.	___	___
5A). The bru**sh** **sh**op is where we buy the horse supplies.	___	___
5B). That **sh**op is where we bought the red bru**sh.**	___	___
6A). We like to poli**sh** **sh**oes.	___	___
6B). The shoes needed brown poli**sh**.	___	___

SH Final + SH Initial
Sentence Pairs

Name: Date:

Directions: Say each sentence slowly. Cycle through each sentence pair. Elongate the sh final into the sh initial in the "A" sentence. Emphasize the sh initial in isolation for the "B" sentence.

Speech/ Homework

7A). Mom is going to puni**sh** **Sh**elby. ____ ____

7B). **Sh**elby will puni**sh** the dog. ____ ____

8A). Hu**sh** **Sh**aron, I can't hear the movie. ____ ____

8B). **Sh**aron, hu**sh** because I can't hear the movie. ____ ____

9A). I put the new plate on the di**sh** **sh**elf. ____ ____

9B). The **sh**elf held the new di**sh**. ____ ____

10A). All of the tra**sh** **sh**ould go here. ____ ____

10B). **Sh**ould the tra**sh** go here? ____ ____

11A). The squa**sh** **sh**oes are new. ____ ____

11B). **Sh**e has new **sh**oes for squa**sh**. ____ ____

12A). Ru**sh** **Sh**erry, you're late. ____ ____

12B). **Sh**erry was late so **sh**e ru**sh**ed. ____ ____

SH Initial Single Words

Name: Date:

Directions: Say each word slowly. Make sure to elongate the initial sh sound. Mark the speech/homework block as appropriate for correct pronunciation.

shake

Speech ___ Homework ___

shoe

Speech ___ Homework ___

ship

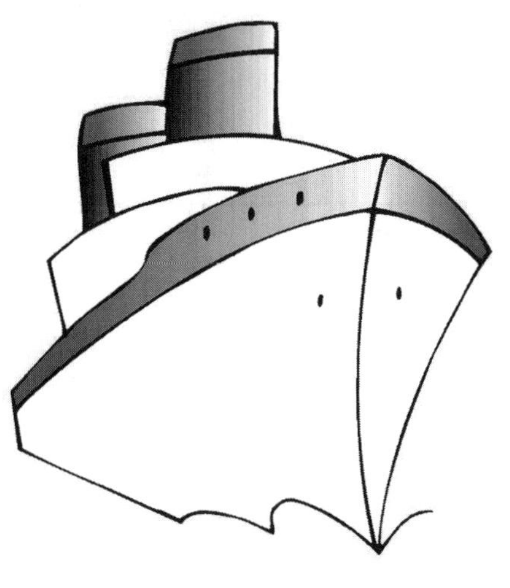

Speech ___ Homework ___

short

Speech ___ Homework ___

shop

Speech ___ Homework ___

sugar

Speech ___ Homework ___

shark

Speech ___ Homework ___

shell

Speech ___ Homework ___

More SH Initial Practice Words:

sheriff
shamrock
share
shower

sheet
shock
shack
shine

SH Initial Phrases

Name: Date:

Directions: Say each phrase slowly. Make sure to elongate the initial sh sound. Mark the speech/homework block as appropriate for correct pronunciation.

Lucky shamrock.

Speech ___ Homework ___

Take a shower.

Speech ___ Homework ___

Share ice cream.

Speech ___ Homework ___

The sheriff.

Speech ___ Homework ___

Wear shorts.

Speech ___ Homework ___

A vanilla shake.

Speech ___ Homework ___

The sea shell.

Speech ___ Homework ___

Bright sunshine.

Speech ___ Homework ___

More SH Initial Practice Phrases:

Let's shop.
Small shelf.
Borrow shareware.
Shout it out.
A sheet of paper.
Electric shock.
An old shack.
Get your shoes shined.

SH Initial Sentences

Name: Date:

Directions: Say each sentence slowly. Cycle through each set, changing the ending for a different sh target word. Mark the speech/homework block as appropriate for correct pronunciation.

Shelly drew a...

shooting star

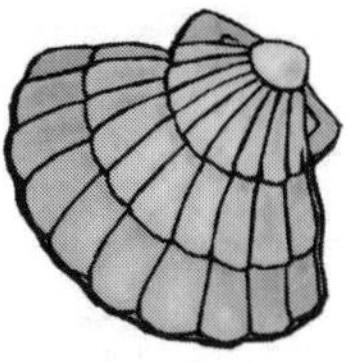

shell

shamrock

Sheila and Shawn shared...

a shake

the sugar

the toy shark

Speech _ _ _ Homework _ _ _

Sherry and Shane saw the...

sheriff

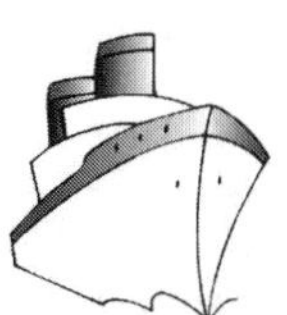

ship

rain shower

Activity: Seashell Color In

Name: Date:

Directions: The instructor should make up a word list. Instruct the student to repeat the words. If a word is pronounced correctly, the student colors in a seashell. If the response is incorrect, the instructor colors in a seashell.

SH Activity: Shapes

Name: Date:

Directions: Fill in the blank with the appropriate answer. Say the sentence aloud emphasizing the word "shape" for more practice. For example: "The **sh**ape is a rectangle."

The **sh**ape is a ____________________

The **sh**ape is a ____________________

The **sh**ape is a ____________________

The **sh**ape is a ____________________

The **sh**ape is a ____________________

SH Initial Activity: Fill-In

Name: Date:

Directions: Fill in the blank with the word from the word list below that best fits. Say each sentence aloud for more practice.

Example:

A circle and square are shapes**.**

1. **We wear __________ on our feet (over socks).**
2. **A __________ says "Baaaah."**
3. **I use __________ to clean my hair.**
4. **We took a __________ to get to the island.**
5. **When playing with your friends, you need to __________ your toys.**
6. **If it is cloudy outside, I can't see my __________.**

SH Medial Single Words

Name: Date:

Directions: Say each word slowly. Make sure to elongate the medial sh sound. Mark the speech/homework block as appropriate for correct pronunciation.

trash can

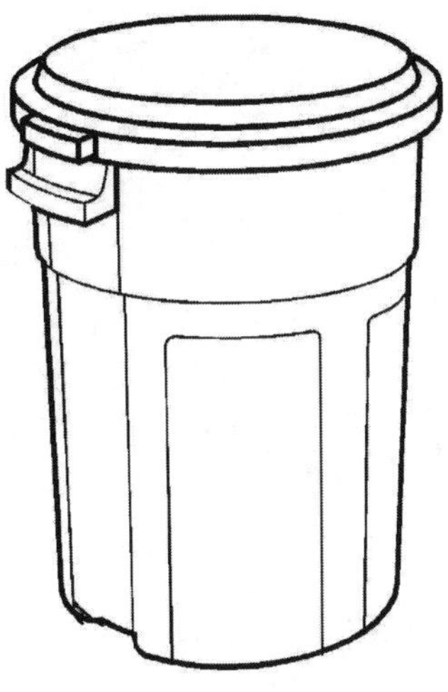

Speech ___ Homework ___

t-shirt

Speech ___ Homework ___

marshmallow

Speech ___ Homework ___

tissue

Speech ___ Homework ___

SH Medial Single Words

SH Medial Single Words

flashlight

Speech ___ Homework ___

Martian

Speech ___ Homework ___

fishing

Speech ___ Homework ___

washing machine

Speech ___ Homework ___

More SH Medial Practice Words:

lampshade
cushion
wishes
usher
station
pushing
cashew
ashes

SH Medial Phrases

Name: Date:

Directions: Say each phrase slowly. Make sure to elongate the medial sh sound. Mark the speech/homework block as appropriate for correct pronunciation.

A tra<u>sh</u> can.

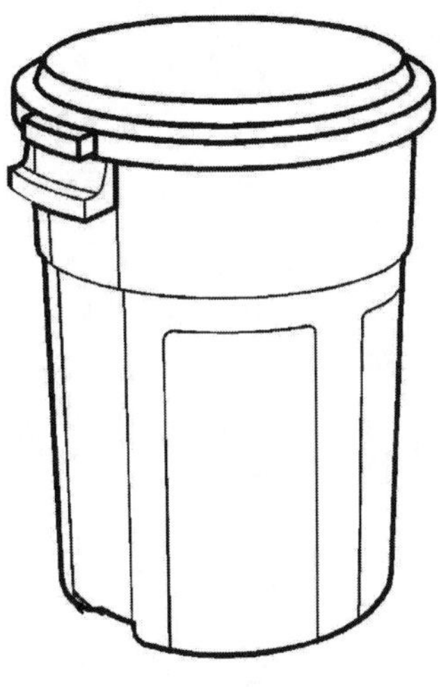

Speech ___ Homework ___

A white t-<u>sh</u>irt.

Speech ___ Homework ___

Roast mar<u>sh</u>mallows.

Speech ___ Homework ___

Take a ti<u>ss</u>ue.

Speech ___ Homework ___

A flashlight.

Speech ___ Homework ___

Look a parachute!

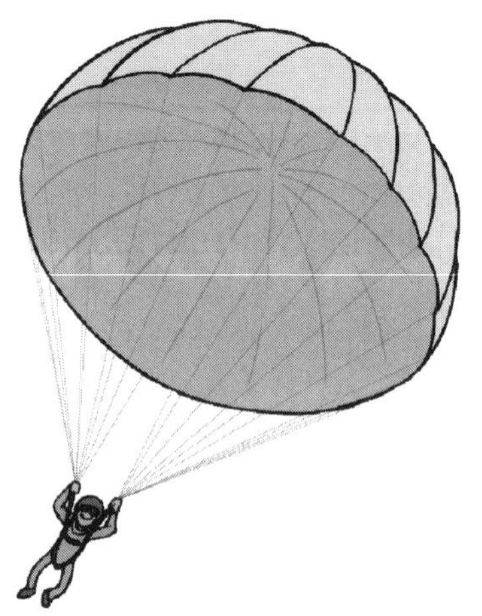

Speech ___ Homework ___

Ocean fishing.

Speech ___ Homework ___

Bring lotion on vacation.

Speech ___ Homework ___

More SH Medial Practice Phrases:

Cloth lampshade.
Seat cushion.
Best wishes.
Church usher.

Railroad station.
Pushing the cart.
Eat a cashew.
Burnt ashes.

SH Medial Sentences

Name: Date:

Directions: Say each sentence slowly. Cycle through each set, changing the ending for a different sh target word. Mark the speech/homework block as appropriate for correct pronunciation.

Michelle went... Speech _ _ _ Homework _ _ _

on vacation

to the ocean

to the cashier

Keisha washed the ... Speech _ _ _ Homework _ _ _

mushroom

flashlight

lotion off

Speech _ _ _ Homework _ _ _

Alicia likes the...

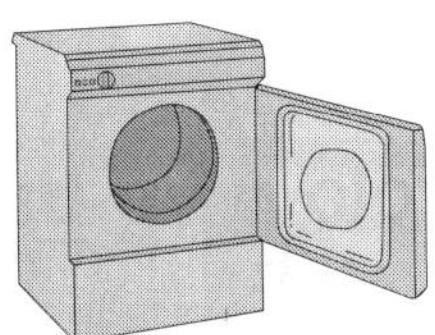

washing machine

Martian

marshmallow

SH Medial Sentences

SH Medial Activity: Horseshoes

Name: Date:

Directions: These word are more difficult to pronounce because of the s and sh and sh and z combinations. Say each word slowly. Color in a horseshoe for each word correctly pronounced.

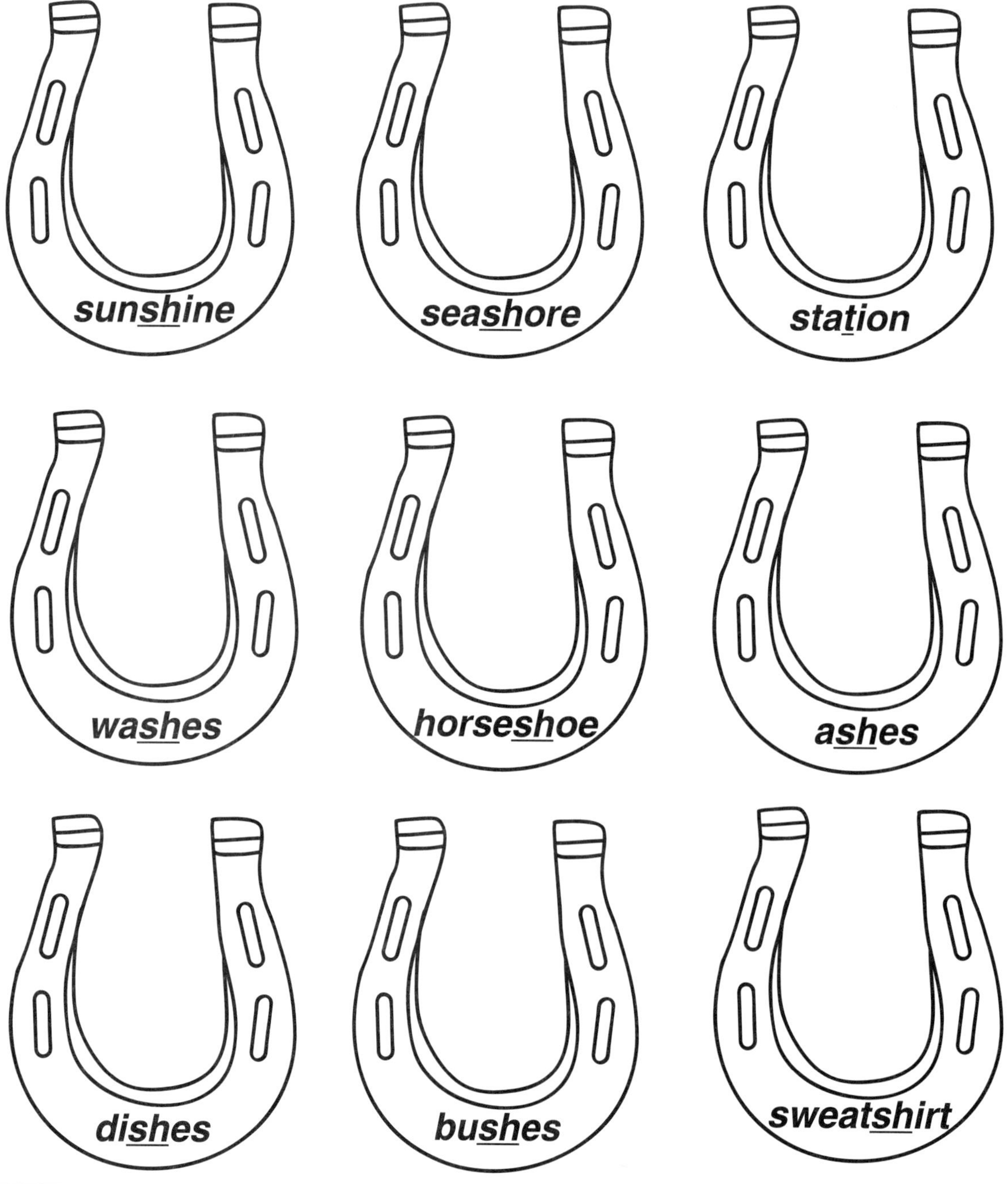

Activity: Mushroom Color In

Name: Date:

Directions: The instructor should make up a word list. Instruct the student to repeat the words. If a word is pronounced correctly, the student colors in a mushroom. If the response is incorrect, the instructor colors in a mushroom.

SH Medial Activity: Martians & Spaceships

Name: Date:

Directions: Identify each picture as "Martian" or a "spaceship." Say the name of each and write it in the space provided.

SH Final Single Words

Name: Date:

Directions: Say each word slowly. Make sure to elongate the final sh sound. Mark the speech/homework block as appropriate for correct pronunciation.

paintbrush

Speech ___ Homework ___

crash

Speech ___ Homework ___

fish

Speech ___ Homework ___

trash

Speech ___ Homework ___

dish

Speech ___ Homework ___

wash

Speech ___ Homework ___

polish

Speech ___ Homework ___

push

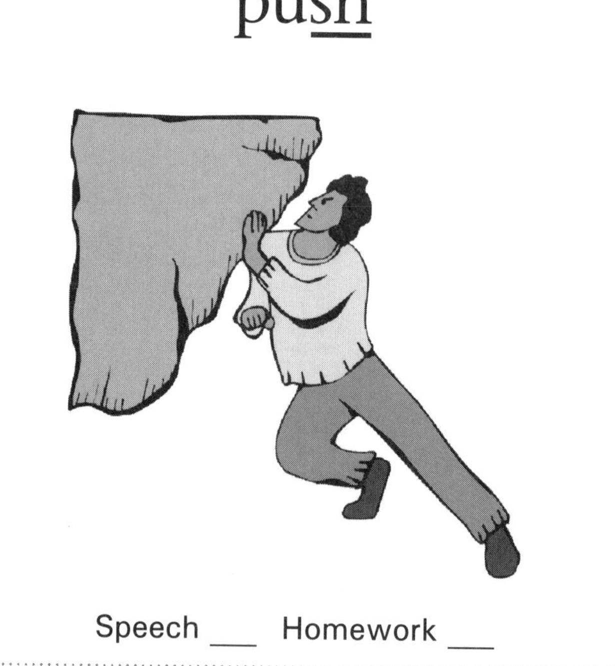

Speech ___ Homework ___

More SH Final Practice Words:

licorice
wish
leash
mesh
mash
lush
flash
toothbrush

SH Final Phrases

Name: Date:

Directions: Say each word slowly. Make sure to elongate the final sh sound. Mark the speech/homework block as appropriate for correct pronunciation.

A cleaning brush.

Speech ___ Homework ___

Pull the leash.

Speech ___ Homework ___

Push the cart.

Speech ___ Homework ___

A pretty fish.

Speech ___ Homework ___

Wash the car.

Speech ___ Homework ___

A dish for food.

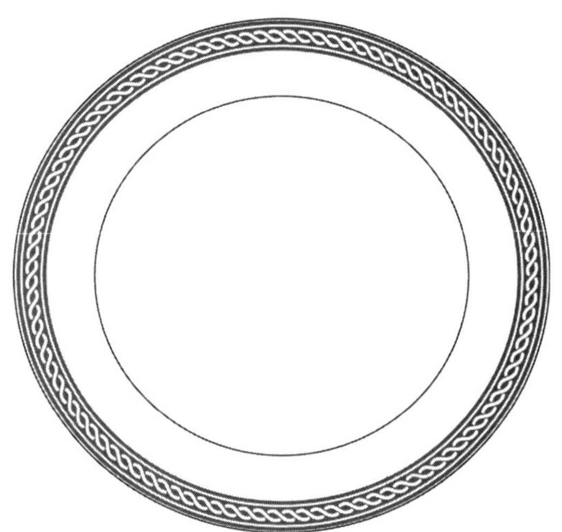

Speech ___ Homework ___

Make a wish.

Speech ___ Homework ___

Eat licorice.

Speech ___ Homework ___

More SH Final Practice Phrases:

Lots of trash.
A big crash.
A wet paint brush.
The satellite dish.
Nail polish.
Give it a good push.
Turn on the flash.
The mesh netting.

SH Final Sentences

Name: Date:

Directions: Say each sentence slowly. Cycle through each set, changing the ending for a different sh target word. Mark the speech/homework block as appropriate for correct pronunciation.

Josh used the... Speech _ _ _ Homework _ _ _

paintbrush leash polish

Nash will... Speech _ _ _ Homework _ _ _

push the cart fish wash the car

Speech _ _ _ Homework _ _ _

Ash saw the...

crash fish flash

SH Final Sentences

SH Final Activity: Matching

Name: Date:

Directions: Circle the picture that belongs with the first one. Say each word for practice. Hint: The words that belong together are more difficult because of the s + sh combination.

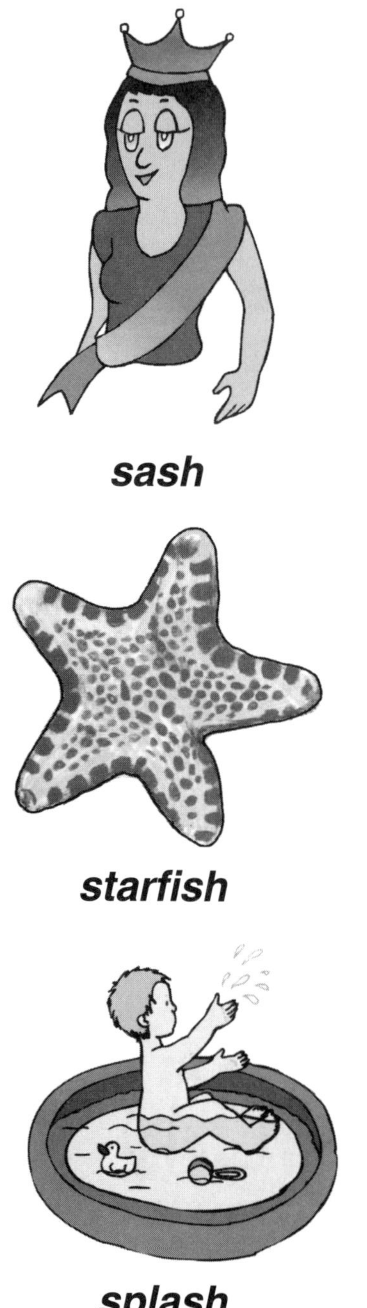

sash

starfish

splash

SH Final Activity: What Doesn't Belong?

Name: Date:

Directions: Circle the picture that doesn't belong in each group. For practice, say the word that each picture represents.

SH Final Activity: Let's Go Fishing

Name: Date:

Directions: Let's catch some fish! Which fish have sh words on them? Color in the fish that have sh words. Say the word aloud for practice.

CHAPTER 8:

The Entire World™ of... Medial & Final ZH

ZH Teaching Tool

The /ʒ/ or zh phoneme, as in the words mea***s***ure or bei***ge***, is the least used consonant in the English language. It is the voiced cognate of sh. It is produced exactly the same as sh with the exception that the zh sound is voiced. The zh phoneme like sh is a continuant sibilant fricative consonant.

To produce zh, the tongue tip points to, but does not touch, the hard palate or "roof of the mouth." In some cases, the tongue tip may be pointing to the alveolar ridge, which is the gum line behind the upper central incisors. The tongue should be curled back and slightly tensed to press against the sides of the upper back teeth.

The air stream is emitted centrally and is forced out over the tongue and through the teeth.

The lips are rounded and slightly protruded or pushed out. The corners of the mouth may also be tightened. *The vocal cords vibrate.*

Production of this sound is similiar to /z/ production. If the student has a frontal or lateral lisp, then proper production of /s/ and /z/ should be attained before attempting to correct sh and zh.

Of note, there are no initial zh words in English and only a limited amount of zh final words. The number of medial zh words is also limited. Considering the vocabulary level of young students, most of these words will not even appear in their speech. In fact a deficiency with zh might not even be detected due to these limitations.

Both medial and final words are included in this chapter for practice and consistency. We've tried to include words with the most tangible context, though a few words that are age-appropriate may appear for your particular student. Take the opportunity to introduce new vocabulary words to increase stimulable practice words.

The key for successful production of zh after attaining sh is the emphasis on good modeling and ear training.

Therapeutic Tips for ZH

Involve as many senses as possible when teaching a student to correct an articulation/phonological disorder. Different modalities all contribute to a successful learning situation. Visual and tactile stimuli reinforce and complement auditory cueing techniques.

The following are a few ideas to try with your students. We encourage you to develop some of your own. Most importantly, use all of the tips simultaneously for maximum impact.

Auditory Tips

Refer to zh as the "airplane" or "motorboat" sound. Model the sound for the student to mimic one of these sounds. Reinforce by repeating the sound at the beginning and end of each therapy session.

Practice the auditory contrast: *th, z, zh.* Voice the "th" and instruct the student to say this combination repeatedly. Speed-up as the student is capable, but don't lose accuracy. This exercise moves the tongue in sequence from the anterior to the posterior position. Combine it with a visual cue of the instructor's hand moving back to indicate the gradual withdrawal of the tongue to the back of the mouth.

Ear training with zh is especially important, due to the limited exposure the student has with this phoneme. Read the target words or stories with the target words to the student. Instruct him to raise his hand or identify the target sound when he hears the sound. It might be helpful to point out that zh is at a lower frequency than /z/ words. Getting the student used to hearing the correct sound is the goal.

Visual Tips

Use a mirror so the student can see proper mouth, tongue, and lip positioning. Model the zh sound and instruct the student to mimic your mouth positioning. Pay particular attention to the tongue tip movement and the lip differences between z and zh.

Use hand gestures to indicate the retracted and heightened positioning of the tongue during exercises.

Tactile Tips

If the student is having difficulty with the voiced nature of the sound, review the differences of a voiced versus voiceless sounds. Model the sound with the student's hand on your voice box, then instruct him to place his hand on his throat to feel the vibration. Encourage him to make the sound in an easy, relaxed manner. Using the student's hand to feel the vibration of voicing provides an additional sensation to cue the proper sound production.

Use "The Airplane Sound" worksheet found on the following page. Refer to the zh sound as the "airplane" sound. Instruct the student to make the sound and trace the flight of the airplane with his finger. Color in the airplane for additional tactile stimulation.

For medial and final single word and phrase worksheets starting on page 187, instruct the student to color in the pictures. Also, cut the pictures out and arrange them into a booklet or use as flash cards for games and memory exercises. (See page 36.)

Remediation Tricks

1. If the student can say sh words, but not zh words, ask him to say sh words to gain kinesthetic awareness of where his tongue is and what it feels like to produce the sound. Once sh is attained with confidence, instruct the student to "turn on" his voice box (vocal cords) and feel his neck for the vibration of the vocal cords.

2. Model /i/, as in "s**ee**" and "k**ey**." Instruct the student to raise the tongue and back, *turn on the voice,* and keep the air flowing. As the tongue is moved into position, the zh should emerge.

3. Try generating a zh from /d/. Instruct the student to make a sustained "deee" and protrude the lips slightly. The zh should appear as the tongue is drawn backward.

4. Use a voiced /r/. Instruct the student to make an /r/ (e.g. red). Hold the /rrrr/ and clench teeth till they almost touch. Move the tongue backward and slightly protrude the lips, while maintaining airflow. The zh should emerge.

5. If the student's tongue is protruding during production so that the voiced th is substituted for the zh, then the student has a lisp disorder. Review the tips and techniques for frontal and lateral lisps in ***The Entire World of S & Z™ Instructional Workbook.***

The Airplane Sound

Name: Date:

Directions: Model the airplane sound for the student to approximate zh. Instruct the student to make the sound while tracing the flight of the airplane with a finger. Color in the airplanes for additional tactile and visual stimulation.

zhhh

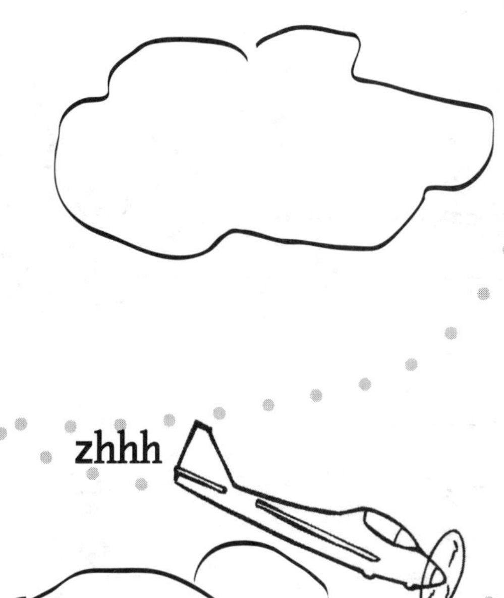

ZH Activity: Motorboat

Name: Date:

Directions: Model the motorboat sound for the student to approximate zh. Instruct the student to make the sound. Use tactile cues, such as placing a hand on the voice box if necessary. Color in the picture of the motorboat.

ZH Medial Single Words

Name: Date:

Directions: Say each word slowly. Make sure to elongate the medial zh sound. Mark the speech/homework block as appropriate for correct pronunciation.

treasure

Speech ___ Homework ___

collision

Speech ___ Homework ___

television

Speech ___ Homework ___

cashmere

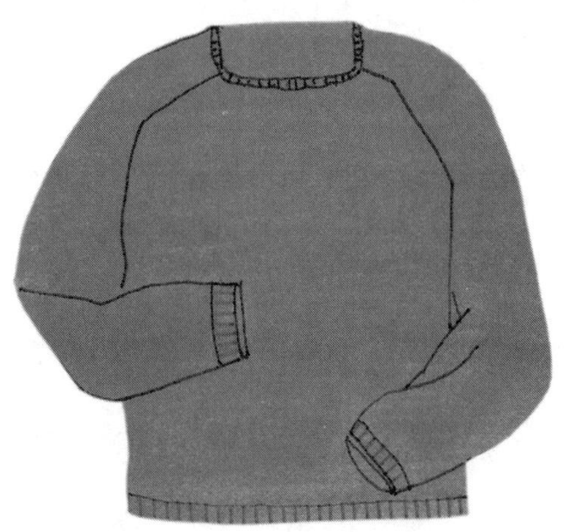

Speech ___ Homework ___

ZH Medial Single Words

Asia

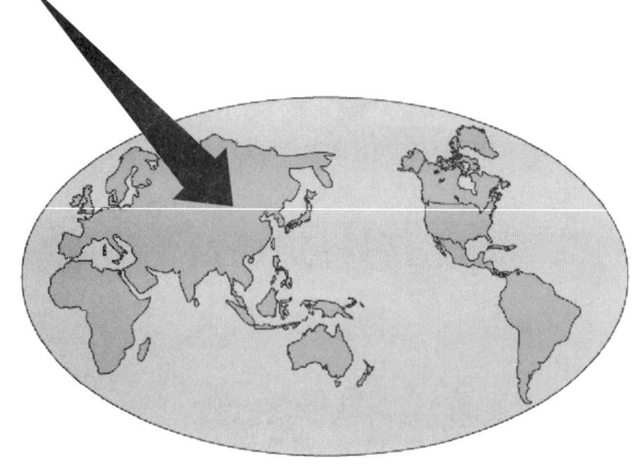

Speech ___ Homework ___

measure

Speech ___ Homework ___

explosion

Speech ___ Homework ___

vision

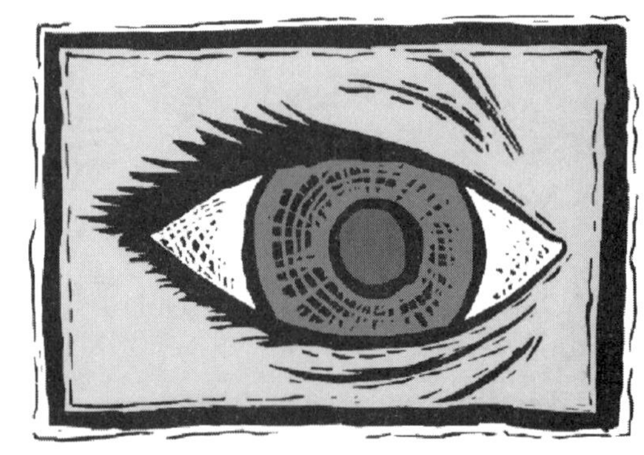

Speech ___ Homework ___

More ZH Medial Practice Words:

division
leisure
decision
casual

pleasure
exposure
azure

ZH Medial Phrases

Name: Date:

Directions: Say each phrase slowly. Make sure to elongate the medial zh sound. Mark the speech/homework block as appropriate for correct pronunciation.

Treasure hunt.

Speech ___ Homework ___

A bad collision.

Speech ___ Homework ___

Turn off the television.

Speech ___ Homework ___

A cashmere sweater.

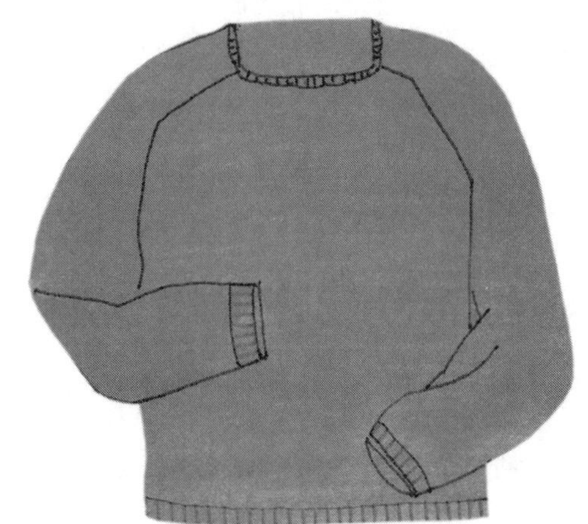

Speech ___ Homework ___

Go to Asia.

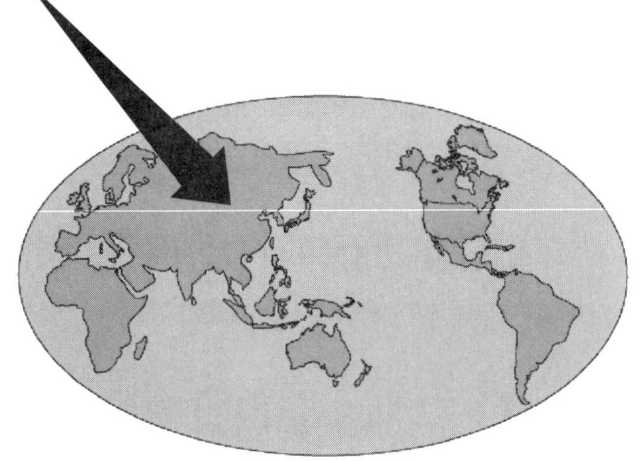

Speech ___ Homework ___

Measuring cup.

Speech ___ Homework ___

A big explosion.

Speech ___ Homework ___

Good vision.

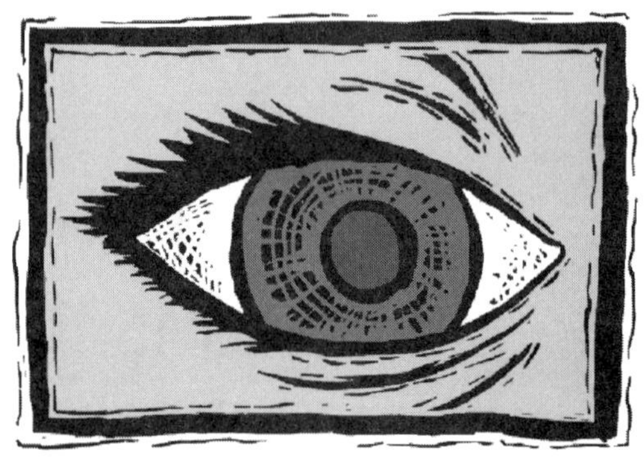

Speech ___ Homework ___

More ZH Medial Practice Phrases:

Long division.
Leisure time.
A big decision.
Too casual.
Too much exposure.
The azure pool.
A pleasure trip.

ZH Medial Sentences

Name: Date:

Directions: Say each sentence slowly. Cycle through each set, changing the ending for a different zh target word. Mark the speech/homework block as appropriate for correct pronunciation.

Sue went...

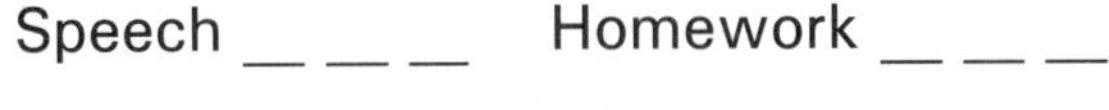

on a treasure hunt

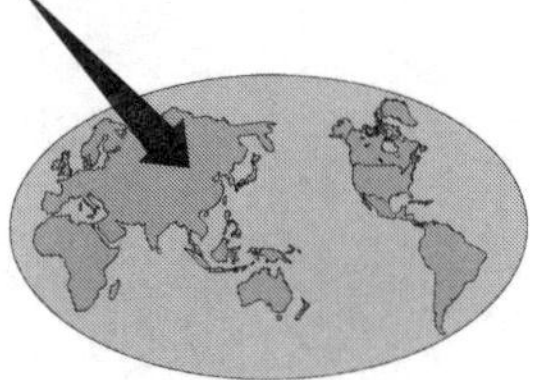

to Asia

on television

Bobby likes...

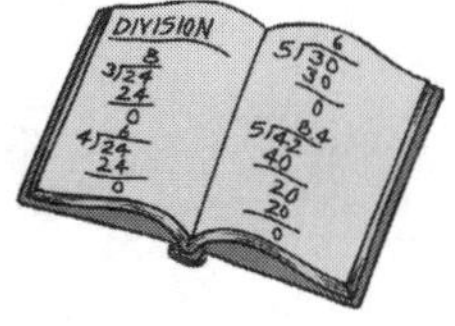

doing division

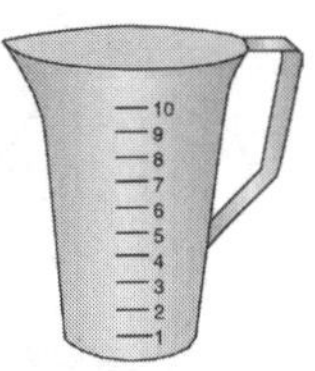

to measure

leisure time

Speech _ _ _ Homework _ _ _

Beth will make the...

decision

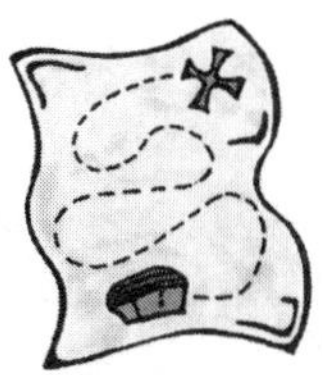

treasure map

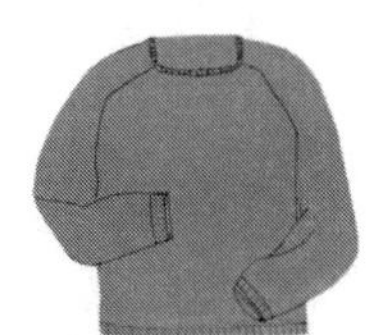

cashmere sweater

ZH Medial Sentences

ZH Medial Activity: Treasure Map

Name: Date:

Directions: Get the treasure by following the treasure map. How do you get the treasure? Make up a story describing how you get the treasure. Use the three words shown in the story. Start the story by saying: "While searching for the trea<u>s</u>ure with my trea<u>s</u>ure map..."

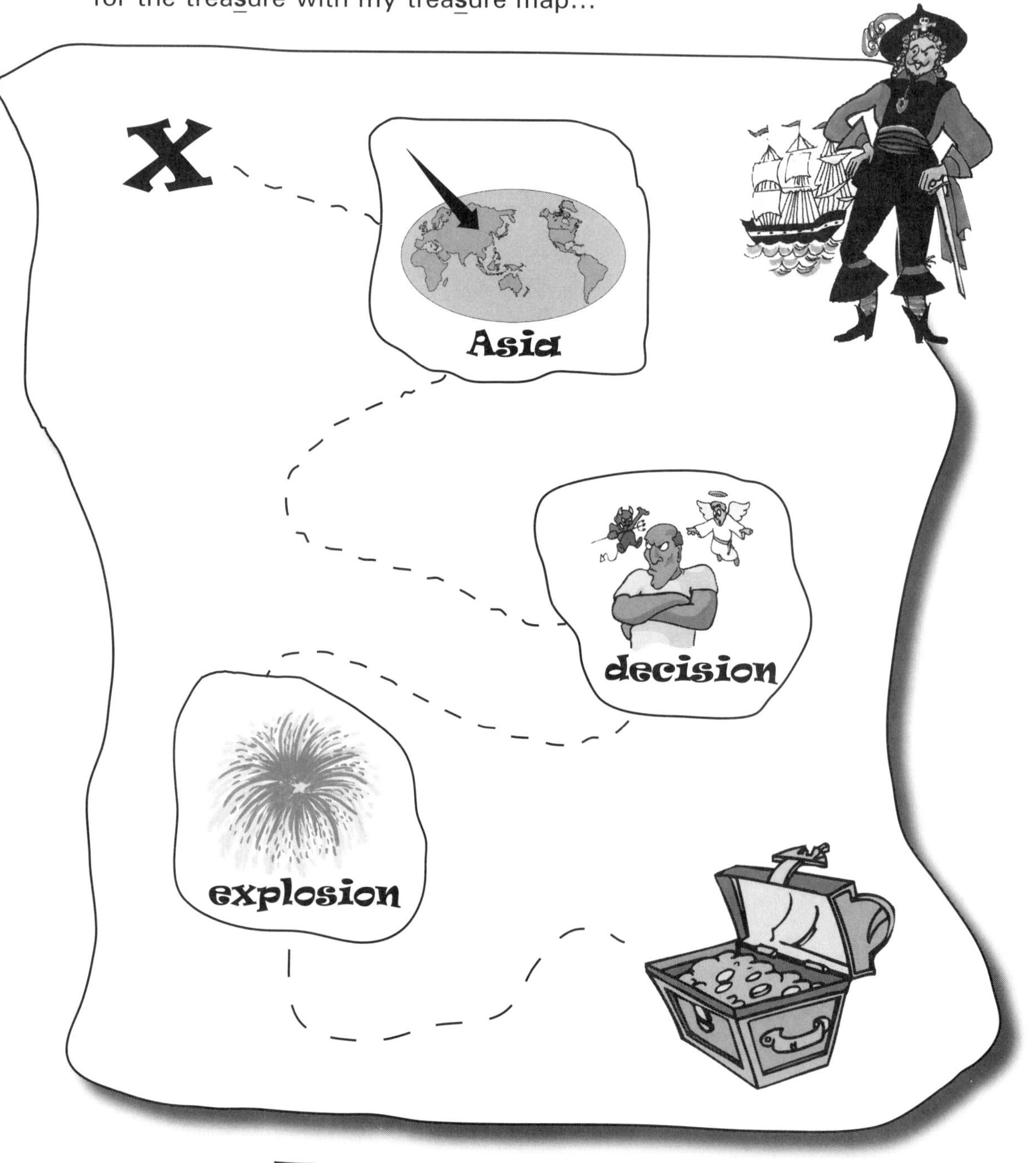

Treasure Map

ZH Medial Activity: Television

Name: Date:

Directions: What's your favorite show on television? Draw a picture of your favorite television show. Say the phrase, "When I make a decision to watch television, my favorite television show is..."

ZH Medial Activity: Measure

Name: Date:

Directions: The instructor should make up a word list. Instruct the student to repeat the words. If a word is pronounced correctly, the student colors in one inch of the ruler. Each time the student colors, he/she should say, "I measure ___inch(es)."

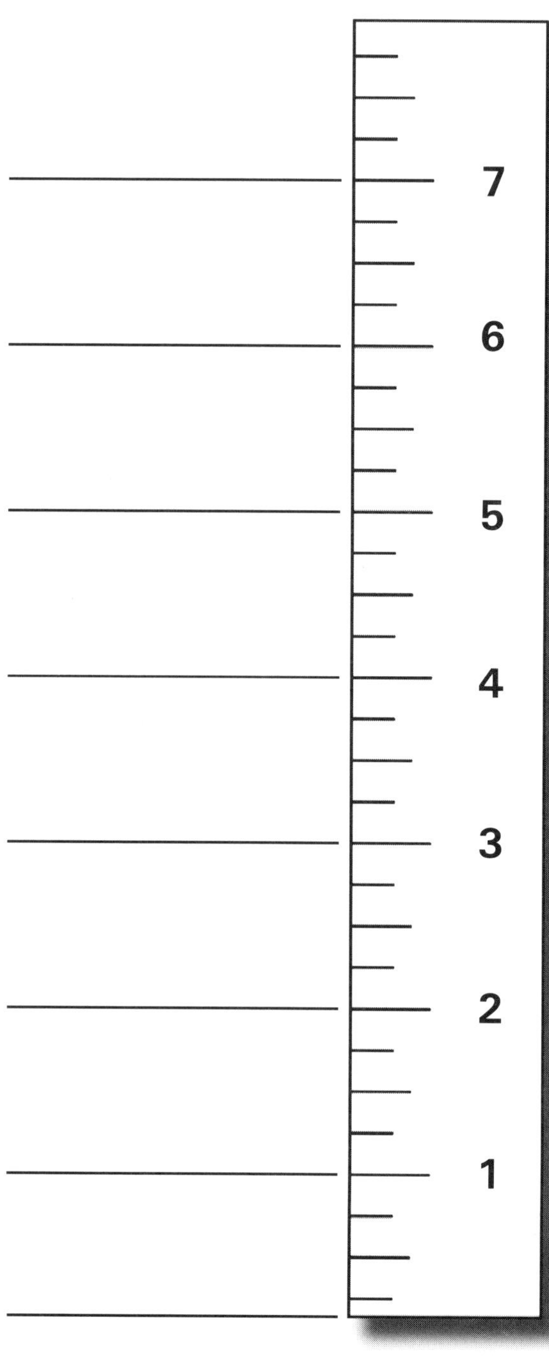

ZH Final Single Words

Name: Date:

Directions: Say each word slowly. Make sure to elongate the final zh sound. Mark the speech/homework block as appropriate for correct pronunciation.

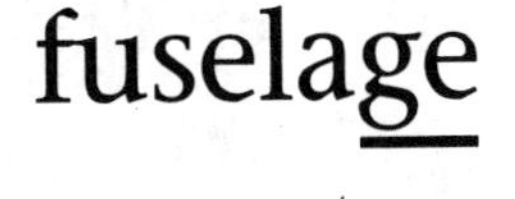

fuselage

Speech ___ Homework ___

garage

Speech ___ Homework ___

beige

Speech ___ Homework ___

mirage

Speech ___ Homework ___

corsage

Speech ___ Homework ___

collage

Speech ___ Homework ___

prestige

Speech ___ Homework ___

camouflage

Speech ___ Homework ___

More ZH Final Practice Words:

entourage
sabotage
massage
loge
rouge

ZH Final Phrases

Name: Date:

Directions: Say each phrase slowly. Make sure to elongate the final zh sound. Mark the speech/homework block as appropriate for correct pronunciation.

The airplane fusela<u>ge</u>.

Speech ___ Homework ___

Park in the gara<u>ge</u>.

Speech ___ Homework ___

Paint it bei<u>ge</u>.

Speech ___ Homework ___

The mira<u>ge</u>.

Speech ___ Homework ___

A beautiful corsage.

Speech ___ Homework ___

Make a collage.

Speech ___ Homework ___

Drive with prestige.

Speech ___ Homework ___

A camouflage bag.

Speech ___ Homework ___

More ZH Final Practice Phrases:

The large entourage.
It was sabotage!
She got a massage.
Watch from the loge.
The rouge makeup.

ZH Final Sentences

Name: Date:

Directions: Say each sentence slowly. Cycle through each set, changing the ending for a different zh target word. Mark the speech/homework block as appropriate for correct pronunciation.

Marge got a ... Speech _ _ _ Homework _ _ _

massage

red corsage

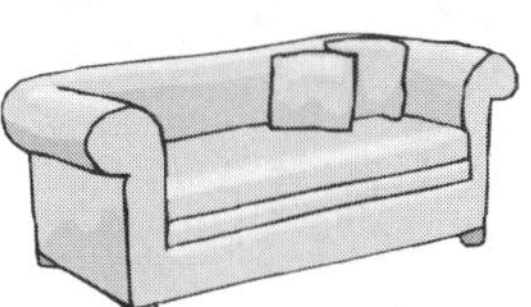

beige couch

Kim saw... Speech _ _ _ Homework _ _ _

a mirage

the camouflage bag

the airplane fuselage

Speech _ _ _ Homework _ _ _

Bill has a ...

a car in the garage

collage

beige shirt

Activity: Collage

Name: Date:

Directions: Make a collage using the frames below. Cut out pictures and paste them into the frames or draw a picture instead. The student should repeat the phrase, "My colla**ge** is made up of pictures from..."

Activity: Camouflage

Name: Date:

Directions: The instructor should make up a word list. Instruct the student to repeat each word. If the word is pronounced correctly, the student gets to color in a camouflage spot. If pronounced incorrectly, the instructor colors in a spot.

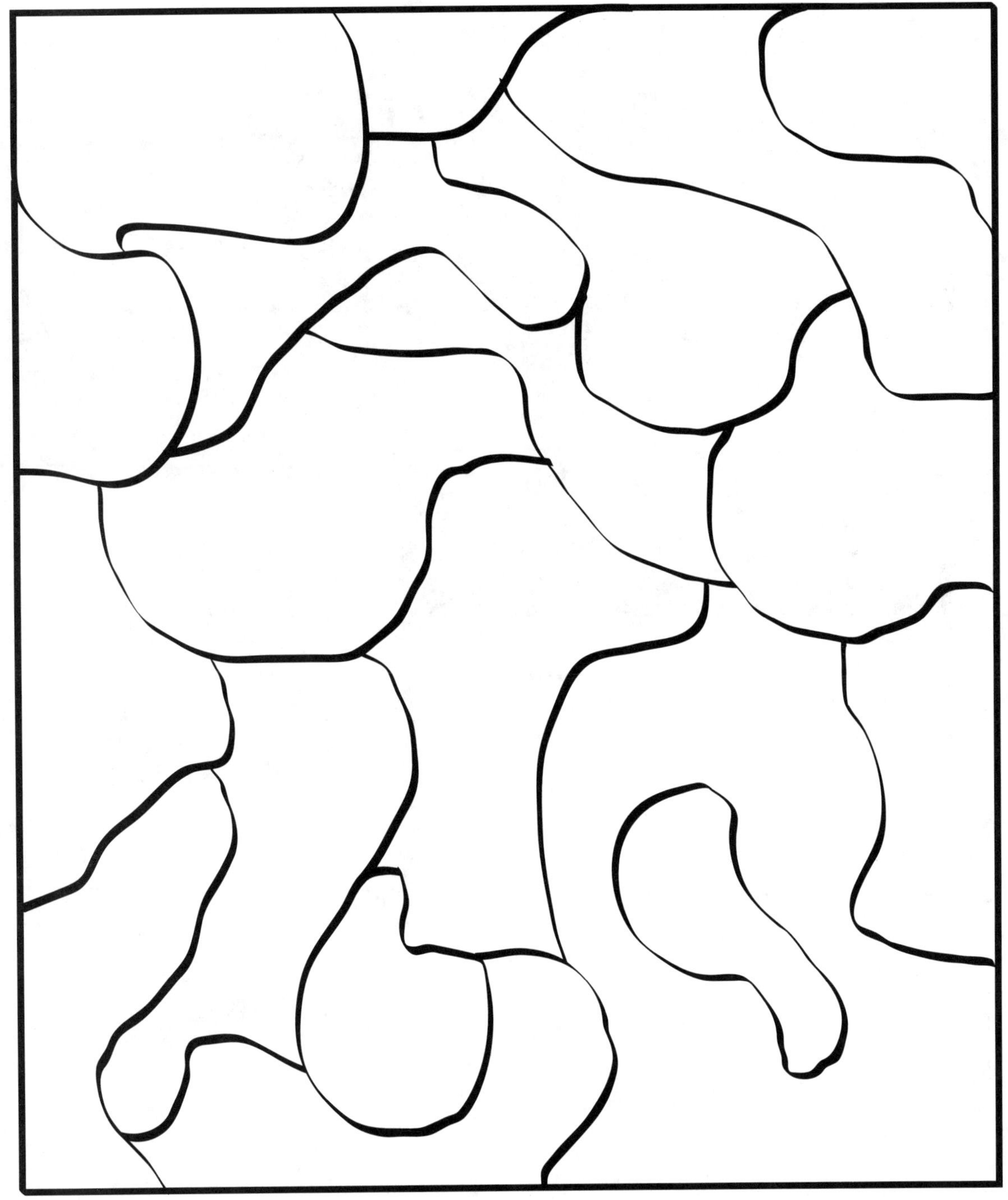

ZH Final Activity: Garage

Name: Date:

Directions: What goes in a garage? Draw pictures of objects that go in garages. (hint: bikes, car, broom). When drawing say: "In my gara**ge** I have a _______. "

Date: ____________

To: The parents/guardian of ______________________

From:_______________________

Subject: SPEECH HOMEWORK

The attached homework sheet is provided for your child. Your participation at home will greatly help facilitate progress in speech therapy.

The attached exercises are a continuation of what we have been working on in speech class. We have been focusing on specific phonemes (or sounds) related to pronouncing the SH, CH, ZH, and J sound(s). The ZH is the vibrating "SH" in words like gara<u>ge</u> and mea<u>s</u>ure. The J is the vibrating "CH" or "J" in words like ma<u>g</u>ic, ba<u>dge</u> or <u>j</u>ump.

The attached worksheet targets a specific variation of the:

❑ SH ❑ CH ❑ ZH ❑ J

Please follow the printed directions for each sheet. Most importantly, instruct your child to read <u>aloud</u> the target words, phrases, or sentences. The more practice the better. Listen for correct pronunciation and put a check mark in the appropriate section.

Instruct your child to emphasize the targeted sound(s). It is important to remind your child to slow down if necessary to obtain correct pronunciation. Repeat each exercise a minimum of three times. Have your child return the worksheet at his/her next speech session.

If you have any further questions, please contact me at_______________.

Thank you for your assistance.

____

Speech-Language Pathologist

Certificate of Achievement

The Certificate is Awarded to

____

for

Excellent Performance in Correctly
Pronouncing the Sh, Ch, J and Zh Sounds

____________________ Speech-Language Pathologist

____________________ Date

Look What's New!

The Entire World of S & Z™ Instructional Workbook

A Comprehensive Approach to Frontal and Lateral Lisp Disorders

- Strategies and tips to remediate S & Z
- Alveolar approximate production zone assists for targeted phonemic remediation
- Case studies on how to implement a remediation program
- Practice worksheets and activities
- Separate chapters for:
  - Initial, Medial & Final /s/
  - Initial, Medial & Final /z/
  - Initial /s/ Blends
  - Final /s/ Clusters
- Save time!
- Get results!!

The Entire World™ of...

21 Playing Card Decks for the 21 types of /r/

Games! Games! Games!

- **27 /r/ Board Games**
- **One for each of the 21 types of /r/, plus 6 carry-over games!**
- **Now available on CD-ROM**

- **20 paired cards in each deck**
- **840 total cards!**
- **Easy sorting and clean-up with color-coded and patterned cards**
- **Now available on CD-ROM**

Games

Card Decks

Order: On-line www.sayitright.org • Call 760-613-6760

How to Order

On-line
www.sayitright.org

Phone
760-613-6760